Practical Marketing for Schools

063653

D1100618

*Dedicated to the
memory of my mother*

Practical Marketing for Schools

Chris Barnes

Copyright © Christopher Barnes, 1993

The right of Christopher Barnes to be identified as author of this work has been asserted in accordance with the Copyright, Designs and Patents Act 1988.

First published 1993

Blackwell Publishers
108 Cowley Road
Oxford OX4 1JF
UK

238 Main Street
Suite 501
Cambridge, Massachusetts 02142
USA

All rights reserved. Except for the quotation of short passages for the purposes of criticism and review, no part may be reproduced, stored in a retrieval system, or transmitted, in any form or by any means, electronic, mechanical, photocopying, recording or otherwise, without the prior permission of the publisher.

Except in the United States of America, this book is sold subject to the condition that it shall not, by way of trade or otherwise, be lent, resold, hired out, or otherwise circulated without the publisher's prior consent in any form of binding or cover other than that in which it is published and without a similar condition including this condition being imposed on the subsequent purchaser.

British Library Cataloguing in Publication Data

A CIP catalogue record for this book is available from the British Library.

Library of Congress Cataloging-in-Publication Data

Barnes, Chris (Christopher)
Practical marketing for schools/Chris Barnes.
p. cm.
Includes index.
1. Public relations–Great Britain–Schools. I. Title.
LB2847.B37 1993   659.2'9371–dc20   92-29852 CIP

ISBN 0-631-188045

Typeset in 11 on 13 pt Plantin
by Pure Tech Corporation, India

Printed and bound in Great Britain by
Marston Lindsay Ross International Ltd,
Oxfordshire

Contents

List of Figures

List of Tables

List of Exhibits

Preface

Andy Harrington sips his wine and outlines his marketing philosophy to the guest sitting across his boardroom table. Flanking him
is his senior management team; around him is the carpeted calm
of the executive suite; beyond the window . . . but wait, something
is wrong.

Beyond the window should be the kind of a panoramic penthouse
view that a successful corporate boss would command from his
office. What is actually there is an asphalt playground, noisy with
children letting off lunchtime steam. And when the bell rings for
afternoon school, the members of the management team rise, make
their apologies, and head for their classroom.[1]

Introduction

This book is designed to help schools undertake marketing effectively, efficiently and, hopefully, as enjoyably as possible. The
reader is exposed to as little complex marketing theory as is practicable and introduced only to relevant aspects of the subject.
Though essentially introductory, the book is sufficiently detailed
to enable schools to competently undertake their own marketing
strategies and activities.

Though a practical book, it does not provide a marketing blueprint: each school's marketing strategy is determined by its own
organizational and market characteristics and the objectives it
sets itself, i.e. the type of school it is, the precise nature of the
market it serves and the end(s) for which marketing is the
means. While a model marketing strategy cannot therefore be

provided, the book does proffer all potentially suitable techniques and approaches from which a school can select, combine and emphasize those aspects of marketing that are appropriate to it.

Value of Practical Marketing for Schools

A number of benefits accrue from marketing.[2] Specifically, it will help a school

- communicate its attributes more effectively at selected target audiences (especially important where a school suffers unjustifiably a 'poor' reputation or image)
- secure a positive image in the minds of parents and prospective parents and other relevant audiences
- create and sustain a quality education service
- improve the quality of educational opportunities by attracting more resources for the school
- extend educational opportunities by maximizing the life cycle of school products and publicizing their existence
- adopt a more systematic and planned decision process in order to realize its stated corporate objectives
- achieve greater organizational efficiency and effectiveness by integrating and coordinating other key management functions
- create a more favourable reputation thereby attracting quality staff, encouraging pupils to identify more readily with the institution and feel less alienated from it

Limitations of Marketing

Marketing, then, offers opportunity for schools to enhance their effectiveness in a number of particulars. It is not, however, a panacea for a school's inadequacies: no amount of marketing will disguise or prolong the existence of poor educational services. Moreover, marketing education is acceptable only if undertaken in the persuance of some recognized educational end, never for its own sake, and in accordance with ethical codes of professional conduct. Disregard of these standards of behaviour will probably render the activity futile or counterproductive.

Contribution to School Marketing

The content of this work is designed to meet the practical marketing needs of schools. It is intended neither to tell heads and governors how to run their schools nor to dictate which marketing strategies they should pursue. Indeed, some schools have developed formidable marketing skills and practices and it would be singularly audacious to instruct them in the subject. Moreover, the book is not suggesting that marketing is a universal imperative to which all schools should subscribe if they are to flourish. Marketing is not, and should never be, more vital than the task of teaching. Simply, it is one of a number of supporting elements in educational management. If, building on the breadth and depth of their educational experience, heads, deputies, governors and teachers gain some additional insight or inspiration from aspects of the book, then its objective would have been accomplished.

Notes

1 Hilary Wilce describing the head teacher, Fairfields Primary School, Basingstoke, *Independent*, 14 December 1989.
2 Recent legislative reforms clearly assign to marketing, either explicitly or implicitly, an increasingly important role in education management in England and Wales. In particular:

The Education (No. 2) Act 1986: created greater consumer choice and competition. This increased parental representation, and required governors to produce an annual report and convene an annual parents' meeting.

The Education Reform Act 1988: promotes a market driven education system in which individual schools will need to sell their product in a competitive environment. This provides for the delegation of school budgets, permits schools to become grant maintained by opting out of LEA control, requires LEAs to pursue open enrolment policies, and imposes on schools a national curriculum and associated testing and assessment policies.

The Education (School) Act 1992: will further intensify competition. This requires all schools to publish their public examination results, including the SAT results for key stages 1, 2 and 3.

The White Paper, *Choice and Diversity, A new framework for schools*, July, 1992: introduces additional performance criteria. It establishes a new national body to distribute funds to opted-out schools; education associations to take over failing schools; a single organization to run both the national curriculum and examinations; and schools encouraged to specialize in subjects such as technology, arts or languages. Some small primary schools will be permitted to opt out, and the opting out process will be made easier.

Acknowledgements

This book could not have been written without the inestimable support and encouragement of many people who gave generously of their time to be interviewed, comment on draft chapters or participate in field surveys. There are too many to name here, but I extend my thanks to them all.

I am especially indebted to a number of senior educationalists, heads, deputies and others associated with the teaching profession: Peter Aarvold, Simon Barnes, Michael Brunt, Chris Chapman, Dr. Ken Hack, Professor Ken Hunt, Ian Jackson, Mr. A. G. Johnston, Phil Laycock, John Lewis, Richard Metcalfe, Malcolm Hughes-Juke, Lionel Morgan, Mr. W. M. Mullings, John Parnham, Professor A. G. Schüler, Mike Tilling and Nick Wrigley and colleagues at the North-West Educational Management Centre. I offer them all my warmest thanks.

I would also like to acknowledge the following organizations for their kind permission to reproduce copyright material: The South-East Essex College of Arts and Technology, The Richmond Schools, Pindar School, Manor School in Nuneaton, Henley-in-Arden High School, the Charities Aid Foundation, Shipston-on-Stour Community School, Birchwood Community School, Pitman Publishing, The Independent, and Coventry Evening Telegraph.

A note of appreciation is owed to staff at Blackwell for their meticulous technical and editorial contributions during the final stages of the book's preparation. Naturally, I accept full responsibility for any errors or omissions.

Finally, my greatest debt is to my wife, Ingrid, for reading and discussing with me the final draft, and to my two daughters for their cheerful support. To all three, my heartfelt gratitude.

1

What is Marketing?

Marketing 'conjures up bucolic images of horny-handed sons of toil from time immemorial setting out from the nearest market town'.[1]

Introduction

In the context of education, marketing means

'the effective management by an institution of its exchange relations with its various markets and publics'.[2]

'analysis, planning, implementation, and control of carefully formulated programs designed to bring about voluntary exchanges of values with target markets for the purpose of achieving institutional objectives'.[3]

'a proven set of concepts and practices designed to increase the effectiveness with which organizations relate to their publics'.[4]

'to cover that which schools consciously do, to identify the needs and wishes of the communities they serve, to publicise the ways in which they respond to these needs, and to promote a public awareness of the quality of the total education which is provided'.[5]

Marketing, then, involves organizing the structure and behaviour of a school around its clients. It is a philosophy or approach to providing education services which is essentially consumer-oriented: it involves identifying needs and wants of specified clients, designing (with due regard to prevailing educational and professional standards and ethos) appropriate education services to satisfy those identified needs and wants, communicating the existence of the education service to clients, and delivering the

PONTYPRIDD COLLEGE
LIBRARY

desired product to them. In this context, marketing is an exchange relationship between school and parent/pupil.

Integrative marketing

Marketing cannot be undertaken in isolation from a school's other management and administrative activities but must be integrated with and underpinned by them. Indeed, one American education-alist argues a correlation exists between the comprehensiveness of integration of the various management activities, of which market-ing is one, and quality: 'Excellence', proclaims James Lewis Jr, 'is a school district that integrates all parts of the school organization – strategy, human resources, capital assets, reward systems, struc-ture, marketing, and promotion – into a cohesive and manageable whole'.[6] A marketing philosophy undoubtedly permeates all as-pects of the organizational life and management of a school (see Appendix A).

Non-profit marketing

In education, marketing is essentially for non-profit. Though com-mercial and non-profit marketing are similar in many particulars, there are important differences between them.

Schools and other educational institutions fulfil pre-determined social needs. In contrast to profit-making organizations, whose continued existence is dependent upon market performance, the legitimacy of educational institutions derives from the social value society places on them and their services, not a capacity to gener-ate profit. Ironically, this factor alone can prove a source of frustration for some schools: educational establishments do not necessarily, in contrast to commercial organizations, increase revenue by making a 'better' product.

Though both profit and non-profit marketing endeavour to sat-isfy consumers' needs, in the case of the former there exists a high degree of consumer sovereignty: where consumers judge a service wanting, based on actual or anticipated outcome, alternative pro-ducts or producers can be sought. But in non-profit marketing, it must be recognized that consumers cannot always exercise choice since access to or availability of alternative products is denied them. Owing to, for example, low parental income, lack of

LIBRARY

public transport, desire for special educational needs, etc., parents and offspring who seek school places might have available to them one institution, alternative provision being impracticable or unrealistic options.

The diminution of consumer sovereignty in non-profit marketing is also evident from the fact that consumers' needs are often consciously subordinated to specified corporate objectives. Most schools, for example, actively pursue certain educational ends which constitute their *raison d'être* and which are at least if not more important to them than unconditionally satisfying consumers' demands.

Key points

1 Marketing is the 'analysis, planning, implementation, and control of carefully formulated programs designed to bring about voluntary exchanges of values with target markets for the purpose of achieving institutional objectives'.
2 Among the distinquishing features of non-profit marketing (as opposed to marketing for profit) are that:

- non-profit marketing fulfills pre-determined social needs
- non-profit marketing operates in a market environment where consumer sovereignty is often constrained by a lack of client choice and a greater importance attached to organizational objectives

Notes

1 Sue Arnold, 'Market Forces', *Observer*, 25 June 1989.
2 See P. Kotler and K. Fox, *Strategic Marketing for Educational Institutions*, Prentice-Hall, Inc., Englewood Cliffs NJ, 1985, Preface.
3 Ibid.
4 Marjo Talbott, *The New Marketing Handbook for Independent Schools*, p. 7. Robert Topor suggests that marketing is: 'The research, planning, and presentation of tangible or intangible products to target audiences in order to achieve planned, coordinated results', in *Institutional Image: How to Define, Improve, Market it*, Washington, DC: Council for Advancement and Support of Education, 1986.

5 National Association of Head Teachers, *The Marketing of Schools* (Council Memorandum), National Association of Head Teachers, September, 1990, para 1.3.
6 James Lewis Jr., quoted in Board of Cooperative Educational Services, St Lawrence-Lewis Counties (booklet), New York, USA, undated.

2

Targeting the Marketing Message

Our customers and our clients we see as the parents, society and industry at large.
We see the children as the consumers.[1]

Introduction

Successful school marketing involves identifying relevant target groups, both internal and external, and adopting appropriate communication strategies to reach them. In this way, a school will maximize:

- its return on any marketing investment made in terms of time and resources
- the accuracy of its targeting of relevant audiences
- the opportunity of finding a target group that will help it achieve its corporate objectives ('mission')

Internal Targets

These include active members of the school community: teaching and non-teaching staff, pupils, governors (including parent governors) and those who provide services for the school from kitchen staff to crossing supervisors. Other relevant internal target groups, whose interaction with the school is likely to be intermitent and generally passive, include parents (excluding parent governors) and alumni. These discrete audience types and the various channels of influence to which they contribute and are exposed, are identified in figure 2.1.

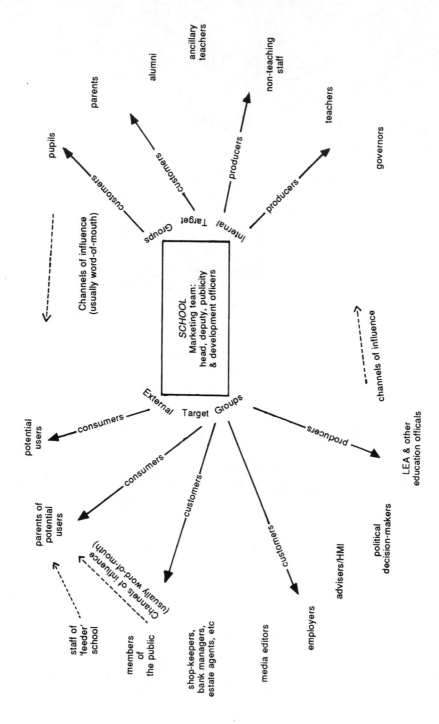

Figure 2.1 Target groups for school marketing

Clearly, the contribution of each internal target group to the marketing effort varies. More specifically, staff are key participants in public relations and personal selling (chapter 9) and fund-raising (chapter 11), while pupils are the school's ambassadors and represent in effect its end product (chapters 8 and 9). For their part, parents contribute to school marketing in a variety of ways: word-of-mouth recommendation, actively supporting school events and offering professional expertise when required.

External Targets

These consist of parents whose children currently attend other schools, staff of[6] 'feeder' schools, industrialists and local employers, shopkeepers, building society and estate agency managers, members of the community, media editors and so on. In fact, all those who comprise the community opinion-formers and with whom the school will need to communicate from time to time in order to promote its marketing objectives. These audience types are also listed in figure 2.1, and their various channels of influences are identified.

Though most external target audience are not potential buyers of education services, they none the less carry around with them a perception of local schools and therefore may exercise considerable sway over parents' and childrens' ultimate choice of institution. Members of the public, for example, can, by word-of-mouth or written correspondence, convey a favourable or other view about a particular school of potential interest to parents. In circumstances where parents lack knowledge of local schools, such informal communication might be critical or decisive to their decision: first impressions tend to be long-lasting. Without doubt, external target audiences exercise inordinate influence over the educational process and shape its products.

Key and Secondary Target Groups

A school's marketing activity is seldom directed toward a single client group, but rather to a number of them, and it has a different and varying relationship with each.

Depending on the strategies being pursued, some target groups are more central to a school's marketing activities than others. The status of any group varies according to the purpose of the marketing message. Where the school aims to advertise a planned open day in order to increase public awareness of its curriculum and facilities (for example, to stimulate demand for places), key or primary target audiences might include the staff and the parents of pupils at feeder schools, and parents with children of school age who have recently moved into the area. In order to facilitate contact with the latter group, other key audiences may be targeted, including local estate agents and building societies. In this context, secondary target audiences might be local industrialists and LEA representatives.

Conversely, where the school's marketing message seeks to attract sponsorship and support for a careers exhibition, then a key target group will be local industrialists, whereas parents become the secondary audience.

Segmentation and the Education Market

Segmentation is 'the identification of numerous sub-groups which make up the mass-market'.[2] That is, it involves dividing consumers or educational products into clusters of discrete homogenous groups according to common characteristics. The value of this activity is the opportunity it affords schools to identify measurable, accessible and relevant target markets.

By using the segmentation technique, 'gaps' or opportunities in the market will be more easily perceptible to the school, i.e. educational needs that are not currently satisfied or catered for will be highlighted by this process. Here, gaps which have been identified in the education market can be plugged, without recourse to poaching.

Market segmentation will also help a school to design education products that satisfy specific consumer needs. In this context, the identity of the consumer can be established and their 'buying' behaviour closely observed. Any adverse or favourable responses toward the educational service can be noted and if necessary modifications introduced in order to match product with consumer needs. Furthermore, segmentation makes possible the targeting of promotional activities more efficiently and effectively on intended audiences, for, as Michael Brunt points out: 'Since the school's offerings are unlikely to appeal to all people, segmentation of the market makes it possible for the school's characteristics to be presented accurately and attractively to people in the ways which are relevant to them.'[3]

In short, segmentation affords opportunities for schools to undertake target marketing by identifying and quantifying relevant markets, designing suitable products for each, and devising appropriate strategies for targeting messages on them.

Approaches to Segmentation

In order to segment an education market or customers and consumers of education services, one or more variables should be chosen 'that will provide maximum variance between segments and minimum variance (bordering on homogeneity) within each segment'.[4] The basis on which a school divides up its market or customers/consumers into discrete groups will reflect, and be determined by, the peculiarity of its market position. Generally, however, a number of major variables are used to segment the school market. These are given in the following list:

Geographic

Region	South east, Greater London, West Midlands, North West, etc.
County size	Under 1 million, 1–2 million, 2–4 million, etc.
City/town size	Under 5000, 5000–20,000, 20,000–50,000 etc.
Density	Urban, suburban, rural etc.

Demographic

Age	4/5–7, 8–11, 12–16, 17–19 (consumers) 20–34, 35–49, 50–64, 65+ (customers)
Sex	Male, Female
Family size	1–2, 3–4, 5 +
Family life cycle	Young single; young, married, no children; young, married, youngest child under 4/5; young, married, youngest child 4/5 or over; young, single, youngest child under 4/5; young, single, youngest child 4/5 or over; older, married with children; older, married, no children under 18; older, single; other.

Income	Under £17,900; £17,901–£20,400; £20,401–£25,400; £25,401–£33,300; £33,301–£41,200; over £41,200
Class and occupation	A: upper-middle class (higher managerial, administrative or professional); B: middle class (middle to senior management and administration); C1: lower-middle class (junior management, supervisory and clerical grades); C2: skilled-working class (manual trades); D: working-class (semi & unskilled worker); E: pensioner & widows
Education	Primary, secondary, higher; public school, grant maintained school, LEA school; university, college, etc.
Religion	Catholic, Protestant, Methodists, Jewish, Muslim, Sikh, Hindu, etc.
Nationality	British, French, German, Scandinavian, East European, Italian, Spanish, American, etc.
Ethnic/cultural origin	White, Black Caribbean, Black African, Black other, Indian, Pakistani, Bangladeshi, Chinese, other.

Psychographic

Life-style	Benefit seeker (hedonistic, active, conservative, value-oriented); sophisticated, homely, etc.
Personality	Compulsiveness (compulsive, non-compulsive); gregariousness (extrovert, introvert); autonomy (independent, dependent); attitude (conservative, liberal, radical); authority style (democratic, authoritatian); leadership style (driver, leader, permissive leadership, follower).

Behavioural

Benefits sought	one specific benefit or a number of them; academic quality, job skills, social life, etc.
User status	non-user (parents without children); ex-user (alumni); potential user (parents with children at feeder school); first-time user (parents with children new to area); regular user (parents with several children at the school).

User rate	frequent – infrequent
Loyalty status	hard-core loyals (exclusively devoted to the school);
	soft-core loyals (devoted to two or three schools);
	shifting loyals (gradually moving from favouring this school to favouring another educational institution);
	switchers (show no loyalty to any school)
Stage of readiness	unaware of the school's offering;
	aware; informed;
	interested;
	intend to buy i.e. enrol (or on behalf of child) at the school.
Attitude	enthusiasts;
	positives;
	indifferents;
	negatives;
	hostiles.
Sensitivity to school advertising and/or publicity	highly sensitive;
	not very sensitive; indifferent.

Sources: Crimp, 1985, ch. 6; Kotler & Fox, 1985, pp. 178–85; Wolfe, 1984; author's research.

For many schools, it is relatively straightforward matching up existing segmentation variables with discrete groups of consumers/customers or markets to whom they might wish to offer their product. Most schools might be able to undertake basic research to identify potential consumer segments or identify relevant target groups from practical knowledge of the education market; school files and correspondence provide profiles of parents and brothers and sisters of pupils which may prove helpful here. Where assistance is sought by schools to undertake segmentation, a number of source materials are readily available (for example: The Market Research Society's publication, *Standard Questions*[5] and Margaret Crimp's work[6]).

Segmentation exercise

To illustrate this process, consider the possibility of introducing a new segment based on an existing variable such as family life cycle.[7]

Young	Young single, no children	Young couple, youngest child under six	Older couple, with child six +	Older couple, no children 18 + at home	Older single children at home

While undertaking research for this book, and taking account of the above, another family life-cycle element highly relevant to education was identified as follows:

> Young
> single,
> youngest
> child
> six +

Given that the consumer described above is likely to be gainfully employed, and therefore in need of child care facilities, schools can offer a product feature which is especially attractive to them: extended school hours, i.e. 8:30 a.m. to 5:00 p.m., coinciding with work schedules of local firms. The Chelmsley Wood area of Solihull has two schools within its boundary that plan to serve this market segment.

It is possible to combine a number of segmentation variables. This is called multivariable segmentation. In the context of target marketing in education, segmentation variables 'user-status' and 'family life cycle' can be conjoined to produce a discrete market segment such as:

> Young couple,
> first-time buyers,
> youngest child
> six +

Possible Target Strategies for Schools

Having segmented the education marketing into various discrete homogenous sub-groups, a school must decide which segment(s) to cater for and plan a marketing strategy accordingly. In other words, a school must decide how it can best target its message at its chosen sub-group of consumers. Three possible target strategies are available: differentiated, undifferentiated and concentrated. Differentiated marketing involves designing different education programmes or products for each market segment or pupil type. Here an appropriate marketing mix is devised for each segment. This strategy has the advantage of enabling a school to maximize its market share, but tends to be costly. In contrast, undifferentiated marketing focuses on the similarities of consumers of education services rather than on their differences. This approach consists of a single education programme or offering which is designed to appeal widely, involves a single marketing mix strategy, and uses a single message which is targeted at all potential consumers. The advantage of undifferentiated marketing is its comparative low cost, but its disadvantage is that it fails to recognize the multifarious needs of education consumers. Concentrated marketing involves directing all the school's marketing effort into satisfying one small segment or pupil type in the total education market by using a single product and marketing mix strategy. This has the advantage of low costs but may prove risky should the chosen market segment dryup.

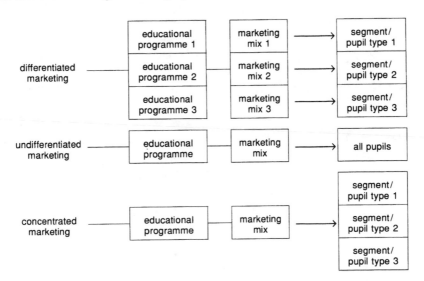

Figure 2.2 Alternative marketing strategies for schools
Source: Adapted from P. Kotler, *Marketing Management*, Prentice Hall (UK) International, London 1991 p. 284.

Of the three strategies, the first and third have hitherto proved the most attractive for schools. Differentiated marketing has been used successfully by the sixth form centre of a Birmingham secondary school, and concentrated marketing has gained acceptance in a number of schools catering for special needs.

Key points

1 There are a number of tangible benefits which derive from carefully targeting the marketing message.
2 Targeting is used by schools for both internal and external audiences.
3 The status of a target group in terms of importance to the school's marketing depends on the purpose of message to be communicated.
4 The activity of segmentation offers considerable opportunities to schools.

Notes

1 Head teacher, Kates Hill Country Primary School, Dudley, West Midlands, BBCI, *Regional News*, 13 January 1992.
2 F. W. Jefkins, *Dictionary of Marketing and Communication*, International Textbook Co. Ltd., London, 1973, p. 62
3 Michael P. Brunt, "Marketing schools", in Tan Craig (ed.), *Primary School Management in Action*, Longman, London, 1987, p. 213
4 H. W. Boyd and S. J. Levy, *Promotion: A Behavioral View*, Prentice-Hall Inc., New Jersey, 1967, p. 25.
5 Alan R. Wolfe (ed.), *Standard Questions*, The Market Research Society, London, 1984.
6 M. Crimp, *The Marketing Research Process*, 2nd edn, Prentice-Hall, London, 1985, chapter 6.
7 Ibid., p. 107.

3

Marketing Action Plan

Perched on the boundaries between Stockport and Manchester is a new college with a ['mission'] statement – Quality Education through Partnership. It runs across the headed notepaper, is emblazoned on the side of the minibus, is etched in the minds of every student and member of staff. It incorporates teamwork and education for capability, individualised learning programmes, a non-hierarchical staffing structure, vibrant links with industry, commerce and the community.[1]

Introduction

In pursuing a systematic approach to school marketing, it is advisable (some might say essential) to prepare a relevant action or development plan. By so doing, a school will derive a number of tangible benefits. It will:

- help identify those attributes or features that distinquish it from rival institutions
- provide a basis for better communication between senior staff, teachers and support personnel and encourage their respective participation and involvement in marketing
- facilitate the development of pro-active rather than re-active marketing strategies, thereby minimizing the need for 'crisis marketing'
- bestow a sense of direction and purpose on marketing activities
- help shape messages to both internal and external target audiences
- highlight organizational weaknesses and problems (the first step in putting things right)
- facilitate analysis and control over marketing problems and activities

Approaches to Preparing a Marketing Plan

The procedure for constructing a marketing action plan, can be either formalized or non-formalized, depending on size and other organizational characteristics of the school. Some have opted for the former approach. North Area 6th Form College in Manchester and John Willmott Secondary School in Birmingham both commissioned independent researchers to undertake detailed studies of their respective market situation and prepare a formal written report recommending appropriate marketing strategies for them to pursue. Conversely, Henley-in-Arden High School and Stour Valley Community School, both in Warwickshire, adopted a more informal approach to planning. Here, responsibility for initiating and coordinating the planning process had been undertaken personally by their respective head teachers, without recourse to detailed market research and construction of a written report. Notwithstanding, both schools have produced sound marketing strategies which have made possible the realization of some key marketing objectives.

The preparation of a written marketing plan, however, does offer distinct advantages: it will assist senior staff and governors to make better informed strategic-management and marketing decisions; and will provide a vital brief which can be communicated to all staff, thus promoting their understanding of the school's objectives (what it wants or needs to achieve), strategies (how it will do it) and their respective role in the process of delivery (how their participation will convert planned strategies into action).

Content of Written Plan

As a rule, marketing plans follow a standard format. The introductory section is designed to provide a brief summary of findings, main objectives and recommended strategies. This part is designed to aid busy head teachers and governors in decision-making. To maximize impact on them, the summary must be 'concise, readable, dejargonised, brief'.[2] In this context, it is important that 'vital questions, and no other, go forward for decision at the top'.[3] The remaining sections of the report reflect the activities undertaken in the planning process and the sequential order in which they are covered.

Contents of school marketing plan[4]

Section	Purpose
1 Executive summary	Presents brief overview of the proposed plan for quick management skimming
2 Current marketing situation	Presents relevant background data on the education market, competition and other aspects of the macro-environment
3 Opportunity and issue analysis	Identifies main strengths, weaknesses, opportunities and threats, and other issues, e.g. need to undertake further market research
4 Objectives	Defines goals and objectives the plan wants to reach ('ends') in specified areas
5 Marketing strategy	Presents a broad marketing approach that will be used to meet the plan's goals and objectives ('means')
6 Action programmes	Answers: What will be done? Who will do it? When it will be done? and How much it will cost?
7 Controls	Indicates how the plan will be monitored

Participants in the Planning Process

In the formulation of a marketing plan, the head's style of management may influence the extent of staff contribution to this process. Whatever, successful implementation of a plan demands that all staff are familiar with it, fully support its objectives and appreciate and accept their individual and collective contribution to its delivery. For this reason, successful school marketing plans are likely to have involved all staff in at least some aspects or stages of their creation.

Increasingly, schools are turning to independent consultants and specialists to help them undertake this work. Clearly, this makes demands on school budgets. While most marketing consultants provide good value for money, there is an inexpensive alternative, without compromising quality: volunteer your school as case study material for project work to final year marketing/business students at the local University/institute of higher education.

Elements of a School Marketing Plan

In preparing a marketing plan, attention should focus on three key questions: What is the school's standing in the educational market

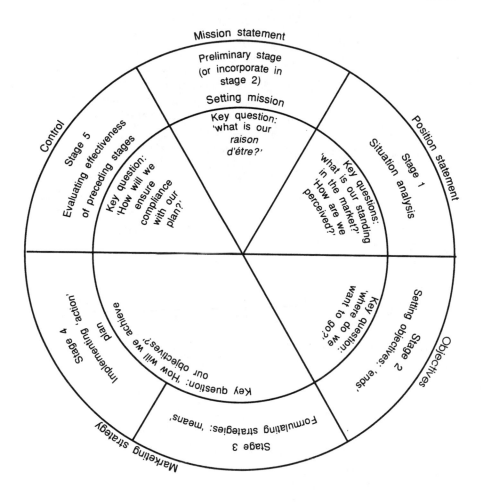

Figure 3.1 Stages in preparing a school marketing plan

place relative to its competitors and how do clients' perceive it? (position statement); where does the school want to go? (objectives); and how will it achieve the objectives? (marketing strategy). In this context, a thorough audit of relevant internal and external aspects of the institution should be undertaken.

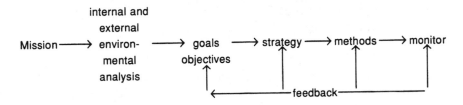

Figure 3.2 Sequential activities involved in marketing planning

Stage 1: Situation analysis

This involves undertaking a systematic review of the school's internal organization and external environment, a process of analysis often referred to by the acronym SWOT: critical appraisal of the school's strengths, weaknesses, opportunities and threats.

The level of detail required for SWOT analysis varies according to the organizational characteristics and circumstances of the school. Institutions that are comparatively small and have sound knowledge of the market and their situation within it, need only a limited SWOT analysis. In this context, a mere ordering of known information into a logical format will usually suffice. Conversely, a large secondary school located in a major conurbation, for example, will probably require a more sophisticated approach to a SWOT analysis. In this circumstance, a number of computer software packages are available to assist in collating and processing relevant data and providing an instant overview of a school's strength, weaknesses, opportunities and threats.[5]

In undertaking SWOT analysis, an assessment of a school's strengths and weaknesses focuses on micro elements in its environment, such as staff, pupils, facilities and resources, accessibility and reputation:[6]

	yes	no
Are there clear signs of welcome?	[ ]	[ ]
Is the entrance clearly signposted?	[ ]	[ ]

	yes	no
Do the staff, and pupils, smile?	[ ]	[ ]
Are the corridor walls in a good state of repair?	[ ]	[ ]
Are there examples of the school's achievements and do they reflect a wide range of talent: practical, sporting, artistic, dramatic, personal as well as academic?	[ ]	[ ]
Are parents encouraged to see all parts of the school?	[ ]	[ ]
Are pupils courteous?	[ ]	[ ]
Are pupils and staff friendly to each other?	[ ]	[ ]
Is pupils' work displayed well?	[ ]	[ ]
Are teachers enthusiastic?	[ ]	[ ]
In conversation, do senior and other staff use 'we' or 'I'?	[ ]	[ ]
In their description of success do they include the sporting, artistic and personal as well as the academic?	[ ]	[ ]
Are parents and pupils allowed to comment on school reports?	[ ]	[ ]
Are there lots of out-of-school activities?	[ ]	[ ]
Are parents shown the library?	[ ]	[ ]
Does it look well used?	[ ]	[ ]
Are there microcomputers?	[ ]	[ ]
Are the school rules positively framed?	[ ]	[ ]
Total	[ ]	[ ]
	(strength)	(weakness)

An examination of opportunities and threats involves looking at a school's macro-environment and covers such elements as the impact of recent government education legislation, education markets, competition and external funding:

What is the size of each of the major markets our school serves?

How is it likely to change in the future?

Where (geographically and by major consumer groupings) are these markets now, and where will they be in the future?

What proportion of demand in each of these markets is available to our school, and what proportion is satisfied by competitors?

Does LMS offer opportunities or pose a threat to the school's future?

Does the national curriculum and other recent government initiatives offer opportunities?

Who are our main competitors and do they pose a threat to the school?

What are our competitors' strengths and weaknesses?

What will be the main sources of competition in the future?

What are our major competitors' goals, objectives and strategies?

Which key factors have resulted in the present competitive position in education?

Do we have adequate numbers of staff, especially in shortage subjects?

Do they possess all necessary skills?

Do we have resources/facilities to meet the training needs of our staff?

Is morale high?

Are they loyal and committed?

Are they flexible and responsive to change?

Is the school adequately resourced?

Are funding arrangements sufficiently flexible?

Are there likely to be opportunities in the foreseeable future to increase funding?

Is demand for places buoyant?

Is this likely to change in the future?

What sort of reputation does the school have *vis-à-vis* competitors?

Do parents, pupils and members of local community perceive the school in positive or negative terms?

Where a more comprehensive appraisal is sought of a school's 'situation', account might be taken also of the discussion in chapter 8, which deals with the topic of image-building. This latter activity will enable a school to ascertain how others perceive it; the SWOT analysis focuses on a school's self-perception of its strengths, weaknesses, opportunities and threats.

Stage 2: Setting objectives: 'ends'

When complete, the situation analysis provides a sound foundation for establishing 'mission' statement, constructing realistic and attainable objectives and goals and formulating strategies. Here, all three elements must be tightly integrated. The life-span of each element does, however, vary.

Mission statement   This is sometimes constructed at the inception of the planning process. Mission statements of the kind quoted at the beginning of this chapter permeate all aspects of a school's organization and working life and conjoin its staff in a shared sense of purpose, direction and opportunity, ultimately influencing clients' perception of it. A school's corporate mission is its *raison d'être*. It provides a consistent theme in all it does; it is the bedrock of its existence.

Essentially, mission statements are, owing to their generalized nature, non-quantifiable and therefore unmeasurable. As a rule, such statements are usually relatively long term, though sometimes subject to review following subsequent re-appraisal of the school's environment and resource situation.

Goals and objectives   A school's mission will fail unless supported by appropriate goals and objectives. Both must be set within the context of the mission. In contrast to the latter, they are quantifiable and as such provide a basis against which future performance can be measured. Objectives are long-term ends towards which the marketing activities are directed; goals are short-term ends.[7]

	life-span	*author*
mission	5 years or more	head teacher; governors
objective	long term 1–5 years	head teacher and other senior staff
goal	short term annual	senior staff; all staff

A school's goals and objectives must be clear, appropriate and attainable, and they must be communicated to all staff. It is important that the school possesses the necessary organizational structure and culture to make communication possible and encourage a receptive and flexible response to the plan from staff.

Stage 3: Strategies: 'means'

While goals and objectives are about specific, identifiable ends, strategies are about means: the broad principals and methods by which the school expects to achieve its objectives and goals in a target market. But set goals and objectives are obtainable only if underpinned by sound strategies: they must enjoy institutional support, attract adequate resources, and in the context of marketing mix decisions, be relevant to education.

In designing strategies, full account must be taken of findings from the situation analysis. Where one or more discrete market segments is targeted, an appropriate marketing mix must be devised for each segment.

Marketing mix concept The marketing mix comprises those 'elements capable of manipulation and variation in order to improve the effectiveness of marketing programmes'[8] and consists of a 'set of marketing tools that the [school] uses to pursue its . . . goals and objectives in the target market'.[9] Essentially, the concept refers to the various marketing components (and the quantities of each) that are needed to implement a marketing strategy. It also determines when and where in the marketing process each element will be used.

In their most basic form, these are the constituents of the mix, often referred to as the 4 Ps:

- Product
- Price
- Place
- Promotion

Here each constituent can be further divided into a number of discrete activities which must be adjusted to meet the school's marketing and competitive position. The list below identifies each of the mix elements and the various activities with which they are associated.

Product	quality of educational experience
	special tangible features of school
Price	scholarships
	free or assisted places
	fee discounts
	payment facilities

Place	geographical and physical location
	environment and atmosphere
	accessibility and availability
	delivery
Promotion	corporate publicity
	product and corporate advertising
	personal selling

Relevant marketing mix for schools   A school should select a mix that will support and reinforce its chosen competitive position, thus enabling it to achieve its objectives and accomplish its mission. To this extent, a school's mix decision is peculiar to it, reflecting the uniqueness of its organizational and market circumstances; it is unpractical to try to produce a blueprint to suit all schools. However, most schools will pursue strategies that involve promotion almost exclusively (image-building, public relations, advertising and exhibitions) and to a lesser extent product decisions too. Both elements identified here must be integrated and, owing to the relative dynamic nature of the education market (especially since the introduction of LMS), may need re-prioritizing occasionally to take account of changing circumstances.

Stage 4: Implementation of action plan

The mere setting of goals, objectives and designing strategies does not, however, entail action. Four activities should be undertaken in order to convert the abstract plan into reality.

First, the school's organizational culture must be suitable. This requires a structure that can accommodate the demands made on it by the marketing plan, i.e. it must be flexible and responsive to change, possess staff who are receptive to marketing objectives and have necessary skills and commitment to fully participate in its delivery.

Second, implementation of a marketing plan has important resource implications. Funds must be available for the execution of the various marketing mix strategies and to resource staff training and related matters.

Third, marketing techniques and methods must be clearly specified. It is important to indicate which techniques and methods are to be used, how and by whom they will be applied.

Finally, the performance of the various constituent activities of the action plan, i.e. the marketing mix elements, must be carefully controlled and coordinated. The process must be scrupulously managed throughout by senior staff or head.

Stage 5: Evaluating and monitoring effectiveness

Here, the effectiveness of chosen strategies are measured against goals and objectives. Periodic reappraisal of the school's mission, goals and objectives, including marketing strategies, must be undertaken, and necessary modifications made.

An actual school marketing plan is presented in chapter 13. The case study is designed to provide the reader with insight into the content and structure of a 'typical' report. Though a résumé, the plan illustrates some key features and considerations in its construction, including:

- clearly specified goals and objectives
- relevant strategies and methods by which goals and objectives might be realized
- statement of findings of SWOT analysis and image appraisal
- identification of relevant market segments and appropriate marketing mix decisions to target each one
- evidence of cyclical nature of marketing plans, i.e. research highlights further information which is needed (customer analysis, etc.) which prompts further research and a reappraised or updated marketing plan.

Key points

1 A number of tangible benefits accrue from a carefully prepared marketing action or development plan.
2 There are a number of key elements in a marketing plan:
   - executive summary
   - current marketing situation
   - opportunity and issue analysis
   - objectives
   - marketing strategy
   - action programmes
   - controls

3 In undertaking situation analysis, attention must focus on

- resources
- internal & external environment
- competition
- market

4 A SWOT analysis is concerned with ascertaining a school's strengths, weaknesses, opportunities, threats.

5 There are number of prerequisites for success in implementing an action plan:

- relevant organization culture
- adequate resources
- available techniques and method to carry out marketing strategies
- control, coordination and management of marketing plan

6 Marketing plan must be periodically reviewed and mission statement, goals and objectives reappraised.

Notes

1 Chris Chapman, 'Rethinking the 16 + philosophy', North Area College, Unpublished paper, undated.
2 Milan J. Dluhy, 'Muddling Through or Thinking About the Problem Seriously: How to prepare Policy Documents, Present Information to Decision Makers and Maximize the Impact of Your Advice', in J. Tropman, M. J. Dluhy and R. M. Lind, *New Strategic Perspectives on Social Policy*, Pergamon Press, London 1981, p. 244.
3 W. J. M. Mackenzie and J. W. Grove, *Central Administration in Britain*, Longman, Longman, 1957, p. 210
4 Adapted from P. Kotler, *Marketing Management*, Prentice-Hall International (UK) Ltd., London, 1991, p. 73.
5 L. Parkinson and S. Parkinson, *Using the Microcomputer in Marketing*, McGraw-Hill, London, pp. 57–61.
6 Adapted from T. Brighouse, 'Parents' guide for evaluating a school's performance', *Observer*, 13 October 1991.
7 Adapted from Parkinson and Parkinson, *Using the Microcomputer*, pp. 57–61.
8 R. L. Willsmere, *The Basic Arts of Marketing*, Business Books, London, 1984.
9 Kotler, *Marketing Management*, p. 68.

4

Internal Marketing and Communication

QUEEN: Now I am going off to think of a plan. When I return you can tell me what a good plan it is; that is what we rulers call consultation.[1]

Introduction

The success of a school's marketing is critically dependent upon the effectiveness of its internal communication. This process is inextricably linked to a number of key marketing activities, especially image-building (chapter 8), public relations (chapter 9), and school open days/exhibitions (chapter 12). But effective internal communication is essential also to the creation of an organizational culture in which those directly associated with the school (teaching and non-teaching staff, pupils, governors and alumni) or with whom the school periodically comes into contact (visitors, parents) respond to the behavioural and institutional changes demanded by a marketing approach. A recently formulated marketing plan for John Willmott Secondary School in Birmingham, advised that the success of the school's marketing strategy would depend largely upon better 'communication with all members of staff to inform them of the need to change'.[2]

Marketing Decisions

It is vital that all those associated with the school are kept apprised of all opportunities and threats posed by external factors, especially LMS, demographic considerations and recession. Essentially, internal audiences must be informed of, and their reactions sought to, the school's rationale for marketing, the nature of its corporate mission and their respective roles in the marketing process.

The more a school informs and involves its staff in marketing decisions the greater is the staff's propensity to support those decisions and become committed to their successful implementation. Indeed, a policy of genuine consultation which encourages active participation in the decision process will help overcome resistance to marketing and minimize any fears staff might have about it. In order to placate an anxious staff at Pindar School, Scarborough, its Deputy Head convened a number of meetings, to which all staff were invited, to carefully explain the school's corporate mission and marketing strategy and the reason for it. The Deputy Head explains:

> anxieties may be anticipated and to some extent allayed by holding a meeting to outline the new policy. Not only does such a meeting afford an opportunity for staff to express any doubts and to hear of the benefits of a marketing strategy, but some at least will immediately put their minds to work on what their department could contribute . . . The fear of an apparent "commercialisation" of education may well be swept away by their own involvement . . . [3]

In short, a consultative approach requires the head teacher to 'tell and sell the decision, tell and listen to subordinates' views and feelings about the decision, ask and tell, that is, ask for the subordinates' view before making a decision'.[4]

A further benefit which accrues from involving staff in marketing decisions is a probable enhancement of staff morale and increased confidence in the school's leadership. For example, in a recent study it was found that among people who know the goals of the organization they're involved with and who receive feedback on their own role within that structure, a full 90 per cent expressed a sense of satisfaction in their jobs with 81 per cent of the same group expressing trust in management. This compares to 50 per cent job satisfaction and only 33 per cent trusting management in the group which wasn't involved in the organization this way.

'Selling' the Marketing Concept

Though important to involve staff in marketing decisions and to keep them informed about related matters, it is essential also to ensure that the benefits which accure from marketing are persuasively and explicitly conveyed to them. Essentially, it is judicious to explain to all staff why marketing must take place, how and when it will be implemented, and by whom. Hence the desirability of involving and informing the school's internal community about marketing. In this way, a marketing culture is attainable, as is the success which flows from it.

Methods of Internal Communication

A school's internal audience is diverse and account must be taken of this when designing and targeting the message. It may be necessary to use different means of communication depending on the audience and the degree of difficulty involved in reaching them. Moreover, it is important to ensure that messages are user-friendly and appropriate, and relevant to the target group.

Table 4.1 offers guidance on the various methods of communication and the techniques associated with each. An 'effectiveness rating' is also given for each technique. From this it is evident that spoken communication, especially the head's speech at parents' night, open days and similar events, is critically important to this process. Indeed, it is vital to the success of the school's marketing generally that unequivocal commitment and clear direction is given by the head on such occasions.

Table 4.1 Methods of communication in schools

Method of communication	Instrument of transmission	Target audience	Purpose	Effectiveness rating[a]
Written	prospectus	parents, governors, staff, pupils local industrialists, staff & pupils (& their parents) at feeder schools	*assist recruitment* of new pupils and *promote the school's image* by communicating curriculum details; articulate the school's philosophy and policies; describe support facilities and resources; etc.	4

Table 4.1 Continued. . .

Method of communi-cation	Instrument of trans-mission	Target audience	Purpose	Effective-ness rating[a]
	newsletter/ school magazine[b]	teaching & non-teaching staff, pupils & governors	*create sense of esprit de corps* by reminding all staff and pupils of the school's mission, marketing objectives & strategies & emphasizing their respective roles in implementation; informing readers about recent developments, achievements, activities, events, etc.; fostering staff & pupil involvement in school life and encourage their contribution to future editions; etc.	3
	regular circular, leaflet & bulletin	all staff, pupils, parents, alumni	*encourage involvement* in the school & *promote corporate identity* by continual updating on school policies, marketing & PR developments, events, etc.	3
	notice-board	all staff & pupils	*announce important information*, display posters & other relevant visual material, etc.	3

Method of communication	Instrument of transmission	Target audience	Purpose	Effectiveness rating[a]
	letters to home/PTA news bulletins	parents	*establish & maintain formal communication link between school & home* by disseminating information on pupil's progress & development/monitoring of national curriculum; advertising forthcoming school events; distributing of minutes of last PTA meeting; etc.	3
Spoken (formal)	head's speech	parents, pupils, staffs, visitors	*promote and reinforce school's ethos and convey positive image* of the institution by outlining school mission & policies; reporting on achievements & successes in examinations & extra-curricular activities; emphasizing the school's strengths and uniqueness; stressing all that is highly positive about the school, such as demand for places; expounding future plans; etc.	5

Table 4.1 Continued. . .

Method of communi-cation	Instrument of trans-mission	Target audience	Purpose	Effective-ness rating[a]
	interview with head/pupil's form/subject teacher	parents	*induce parents into the school* by inviting them to personally collect their child's report, thereby facilitating discussion with relevant teacher(s) about the pupil's progress, behaviour & aspirations; etc	5
	PTA meetings[c]	parents & staff	*provide forum for reciprocal communication* on all relevant matters	1
	school events: sports days, concerts, industrial fairs, etc.	parents, pupils, parents & children from feeder schools, visitors and other external customers	*promote the school,* its pupils, staff and facilities (outstanding opportunity for marketing and PR) by attracting target audience into school	5
Spoken (informal)	impromptu meeting, in staff room & dining room	all staff	*informal exchange of views and opinions* on relevant matters	4
	social gathering outside school hours	all staff	*foster informal/casual discussion* between colleagues in relaxed atmosphere	3
	inservice training, working groups & formal staff meetings	relevant staff	*provide forum for staff consultation and participation* in marketing decision-making and planning	5

Method of communi-cation	Instrument of trans-mission	Target audience	Purpose	Effective-ness rating[a]
	parents' evening	all staff & parents	*source of feedback* from parents, promote the school's marketing objectives, and correct any misinformation due to adverse publicity	3
	staff/pupil grapevine	not specific	*natural concomitant of school life,* sometimes useful but often source of irritating gossip	1
Non-verbal	general behaviour & attitude of pupils, staff & other members of the school; general ambiance of school	parents, visitors, pupils, members of the public	*reinforce positive external image* of the school; *promote PR objectives* and related marketing objectives	4
Visual	displays of pupils' work, photographs carried in newspapers, notices, school uniforms, state of school premises, etc.	parents, visitors, members of the public, etc.	*outward expression of the school's activity, quality and commitment*	4

[a] Scale: 5 = most effective; 1 = least effective. This is a rough guide only to relative communication effectiveness of the various methods listed. The scale is based on the author's discussions with numerous heads and deputies who were interviewed as part of the research for the book and the evidence in the survey findings in Appendix A.

^b Especially important means of internal communication where school is large and/or operates split site.

^c Low ranking on effectiveness scale owing to general low turnout/attendance.

Key points

1 The success of a school's marketing is critically dependent upon the effectiveness of its internal communication.
2 It is vital that all those associated with a school are kept informed of all opportunities and threats posed by external factors, especially LMS and other recent developments.
3 Actively involving staff in the marketing decision process is highly effective for inducing them into the marketing culture.
4 It is important to explain to staff why the school needs to undertake marketing

Notes

1 Enysham Primary School pantomime. Evil Queen addressing her counsellors.
2 Confidential Report, 'A Marketing Plan for John Willmott School', March, 1988.
3 Mike Tilling, *Press and Public Relations in Education: A Practical Guide*, Sheffield Paper in Education Management Number 75, Sheffield City Polytechnic Centre for Education Management and Administration, 1988, p. 38.
4 E. Chell, *Psychology of Behaviour in Organisations*, Macmillan, London, 1987, pp. 150–51.

5

Understanding the Education Market: Techniques and Methods of Market Research

Introduction

Marketing research is about the 'systematic gathering, recording, and analysing of data about problems relating to the marketing of goods and services'.[1] In the context of education, this includes researching market segments, evaluating the competition, testing the receptiveness of parents and others toward new or modified education services, gauging effectiveness of school advertising, and assessing the impact of image-building activities. Essentially marketing research is concerned with providing a school with vital information 'which will facilitate the identification of an opportunity or problem situation and . . . assist in arriving at the best possible decisions when such situations are encountered'.[2]

While many of the techniques and methods of enquiry discussed in this chapter are highly pertinent to market*ing* research, the focus here is toward market research, a 'branch of social science which uses scientific methods to collect information about markets for goods and services'.[3]

Preparation

Survey planning

Fundamental to the process of market research is an initial statement of objectives in unequivocal and precise terms and a decision on the use to which the research findings will be put. In this way, those responsible for carrying out surveys into aspects of the education market will be better equipped to know what it is they are searching for. Where market research lacks clear direction, the enquiry may become unnecessarily protracted and less likely to yield the required information.

Survey time-scale

Ease of access to sources and type of research techniques used is clearly relevant in gauging the time for completion. A leading marketing consultant for independent schools usually completes within eight weeks.

Research brief

The coherence and soundness of a market research project derives from a clear statement of aims and activities which form the basis of the empirical enquiry. This statement constitutes the research brief and it indicates what must be investigated and the approaches to be used. While every brief is peculiar to the school undertaking the research (since it reflects the school's own unique market position and research objectives), a number of principal elements common to all such research statements can be identified.

Research objectives This is essential to all research briefs. In setting objectives, a school must seek to answer a number of key questions:

What is the size of the educational market it serves and what is its current share?

How do parents, pupils and other clients perceive the school?

To what extent does the school's current educational programme fulfil the expectations and needs of clients?

What is the buying behaviour of clients in the product field?

How is the school judged *vis-à-vis* competitors?

What are the future trends in educational provision and how well is the school equipped to respond to future developments and opportunities?

Market research is intended to provide answers to these and other related questions. Above all it is important that objectives are realistic and clear.

Terms of reference Here, details of the research to be carried out and the nature of the information sought should be clearly specified. In this context, a research brief indicates the sources from which data is likely to be obtained; information relating to the field survey such as size and composition of the interview sample and the respondents to be used; time-scale for the commencement and completion of the report; and the allocation of funds to cover costs of the research work.

Statement of research methods Under this heading an indication is given of the data to be found, where it is obtainable and from whom. Relevant secondary and primary sources should be cited. Reference should be made also to the sample of respondents and matters relating to field work, such as details of the type of field work to be undertaken, procedures to be adopted and how findings might be processed and analyzed.

Presentation of report and recommendations A report of the survey findings must contain a clear statement of recommendations. A conventional layout of such a report can be illustrated by reference to typical chapter headings:

Introduction: Statement of objectives, survey brief/terms of reference
    and methods of research
Executive brief
General survey information
Survey procedure and operation
Field work (1): Organization and control
Field work (2): Operation and survey responses
Data processing
Summary of survey results
Recommendations
Conclusion

Types of Data

The data used in researching the education market are either primary or secondary. Primary refers to data which is specific to the enquiry and 'original material, whether archival or newly researched'[4]; secondary data to that which is generally available and is 'non-original material such as commentaries on original data'.[5] Primary and secondary data are further divisible into qualitative/quantitative and internal/external respectively.

Approaches to Data Collection

Research data are gathered on either an *ad hoc* or continuous basis by the processes of questioning and observation. These processes surface in various guises over the course of the research, through the stages of desk research and field research.

Desk research

This is the initial stage in the market research process and involves surveying relevant secondary data. In this context, an educational researcher might peruse a number of *internal* secondary sources, such as school files and correspondence from parents. Relevant *external* secondary sources might include LEA reports, DES Official Statistics and papers, data and annual census material compiled by accredited agencies such as The Independent Schools Information Service (ISIS),[6] regular fact sheets and newsletters published by the National Association of Teachers, and information produced by other representative associations of the teaching profession. Specific examples of secondary source material include Klaus Boehn and Jenny Lees-Spalding, *The Schools Book* (Macmillan Papermac, 1989). More general sources might include the plethora of marketing data produced by relevant professional organizations such as the Advertising Association.[7]

The value of external secondary sources in promoting understanding of the education market and highlighting market opportunities is evident from table 5.1, an extract from statistical data produced by Birmingham LEA. The data shown here indicate significant changes in the total education market in north Birmingham (as measured by the number of pupils eligible for a secondary school place) between 1989 and 1998. While the market will increase by 3.8 per cent over the next five years, and 9 per cent over the next ten years, a fall is predicted in 1991, 1994 and 1996. To what purpose might a local school put this information? The predictions in table 5.1 suggest that, if a secondary school in north Birmingham intends retaining its market share, an appropriate marketing strategy must be in place in the preceding years.

Table 5.1 Predictions for size of secondary school market 1989–98, Birmingham Metropolitan District Council Education Department (North District)

	1989	1990	1991	1992	1993	1994	1995	1996	1997	1998
No. of pupils eligible	1098	1128	1068	1152	1167	1140	1134	1068	1122	1197
Change (%) yearly		+2.7	−5.3	+7.8	+1.3	−2.3	−0.5	−5.8	+5	+6.6

[a] Figures are for January.
Source: Department of Statistics, Birmingham Local Education Authority, North District.

Field research: Qualitative and quantitative

Qualitative research is about discovering clients' perceptions, experiences, attitudes, opinions, and feelings towards a particular school or educational service. It is concerned with the more elusive aspects of consumer behaviour in the educational product field, namely, those elements of clients' behaviour which are difficult to measure. By using unstructured, in-depth interviews, group problem-tracking discussions and similar exploratory techniques, qualitative research seeks answers to questions such as: What do parents think of the school? What do pupils think of the school's facilities? And what is the school's standing and reputation in the community?

Qualitative research helps schools identify relevant questions and hypotheses that can be subsequently tested by survey using a structured questionnaire. Thus, it provides a basis on which a more detailed and controlled enquiry, involving 'quantitative research', can take place. In other words, the prescribed approach is to do

> enough *qualitative* work to reveal most, if not all, of the ways in which consumers behave in the market and of the attitudes they hold; then to use this rich data to design a *quantitative* study of a sample sufficiently large to allow conclusions to be drawn as to *how many*, and *what sort of* consumers behave and think in the ways shown by the qualitative study.[8]

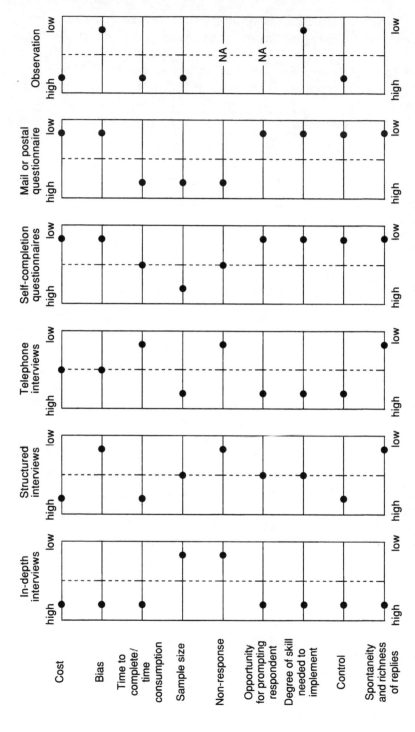

Figure 5.1 Comparison of the management and effectiveness of relevant market research techniques

Though in this context the relationship between qualitative and quantitative research appears to be a sequential one, this is not always the case: quantitative research sometimes gives rise to the need for further qualitative investigations. Strictly speaking, the relationship between them is essentially cyclical.

Data collecting techniques

A number of methods for collecting data are available to the education market researcher: structured or direct interview, self-completion questionnaire, telephone interview, mail or postal questionnaire. In choosing the most appropriate method(s), consideration must be given to two factors: the size of sample from which the market data is to be elicited, and the various characteristics of the research activities in terms of cost, time, etc.

Account must be taken of the total 'universe' from which potential respondents will be drawn. If the universe is, say, five to ten persons, then clearly a postal or mail questionnaire is inappropriate; an in-depth interview or structured interview is best. In cases where the total universe is over 100, then a mail or postal questionnaire is the most effective means of eliciting information from the market. Where the total universe is high, say 500 or more, then a sample must be taken of typical or representative members of the universe.

The size of the universe is only one factor which the educational researcher must take account of in choosing the method or instrument for collecting market information. Other relevant considerations in this process are identified in figure 5.1. Here, all relevant activities are indicated and a general at-a-glance appraisal of each is made in terms of specific criteria, namely: cost, bias, time to complete, degree of likely non-response, opportunity for prompting respondent, degree of skill needed to implement relevant activity, degree of control, spontaneity and richness of respondent's replies.

Questionnaire

This is an important component of field surveys. But the effectiveness of this data collection instrument is critically dependent upon the care and adroitness with which it is constructed and the manner in which it is implemented. There are a number of basic rules which it is advisable to follow in order to facilitate success in this activity. These are described in detail in Appendix B. Additionally, the reader may wish to consult relevant texts such as those published by The Market Research Society.[9]

Model questionnaire: Example of best practice

To illustrate good practice in design, a facsimile of a real-life questionnaire is reproduced in Appendix C. Where appropriate, and possibly subject to some modification, a school may choose to use one or more features of the model questionnaire for use in a market research survey. Keep in mind that where a questionnaire is intended simply to guide an interviewer during an in-depth discussion with a respondent, it needs to be less polished and 'fine-tuned'; but in the case of structured, postal and self-completion questionnaires, the opposite applies.

Using Consultants

Though many marketing and market research consultants specializing in schools report dramatic increases in demand for their services, for most schools they remain financially prohibitive. In this circumstance, three alternative options exist for schools: undertake their own market research; use group or collaborative marketing to reduce costs (see chapter 6); or approach the business faculty of your local institution of higher education and offer your school as a marketing exercise for students. Students of marketing on undergraduate business studies programmes usually welcome the opportunity of applying their knowledge to concrete, practical problems or situations.

Key points

1 In planning a market research project, it is important to

- establish clear objectives
- set time-scale for completion of project
- construct an appropriate research brief

2 Data used in market research is either primary or secondary.
3 Desk research constitutes an initial stage in market research.
4 Field research is comprised of qualitative and quantitative types of investigation.
5 Data collection techniques include:

- structured or direct interview
- in-depth interview
- mail or postal questionnaire
- self-completion questionnaire
- telephone interview
- observation

6 Where a school feels it lacks adequate expertise to expedite all or part of the market research activity, the services of a marketing consultant or alternative may be sought.

Notes

1 H. Boyd, S. Westfall and T. Stasch, *Marketing Research*, Unwin, Inc., Chicago, pp. 4–5; definition also in Fred. R. Davis, *Fundamentals of Strategic Management*, Bobbs-Merrill, Indianapolis p. 163
2 Boyd et al., *Marketing Research*, p. 5
3 Definition of The Market Research Society.
4 F. W. Jefkins, *Dictionary of Marketing & Communications*, International Textbook Company Ltd., Buckinghamshire, UK, 1973, p. 82.
5 Ibid, p. 97.
6 In the USA, a comparable organization is the National Association of Independent Schools which is located in Washington DC.
7 NTC Publications' *Marketing Pocket Book*, which is published by the Advertising Association, retails at £12.50 per copy. This annually updated source book represents good value and covers some vital areas of interest to schools such as demographics and media. A further indicative source is Key Note Publication's specialist reports such as *Guide to Buying Market Research* which retails at £58.
8 Margaret Crimp, *The Marketing Research Process* 2nd edn, Prentice-Hall International (UK) Ltd., 1985, p. 24

9 For example: Market Research Development Fund, Seminar
Proceedings, *Reliability and Validity in Qualitative Research,*
(priced £20) and *Increasing Response,* (£25), The Market Research Society; The Market Research Society's publication
Guide to Good Coding Practice, is inexpensive (£2.50) and provides an invaluable resource, and The Society's publication
Standard Questions is also worth consulting.

6

Group or Collaborative Marketing

Introduction

Earlier, it had been argued that many teachers objected to marketing on the grounds that it engendered unethical and damaging competition between rival schools for the same, dwindling pool of prospective pupils. In circumstances where individual institutions have consciously desisted from marketing, it has usually advantaged those competitors whose concern about such impropriety has been less evident. But group or collaborative marketing offers a practical solution to the dilemma facing those schools who have misgivings about marketing or who simply cannot afford it.

Group or Collaborative Marketing

This involves a number of schools with shared interests and values, who would ordinarily compete with each other for the same market and operate in comparative isolation, undertaking common and mutually supportive marketing strategies. To some extent, this is a logical extension of existing practice where teachers regularly meet at professional conferences to exchange views or share experiences relating to work. Obviously, group marketing is not a substitute for individual school marketing nor will it necessarily eradicate competition entirely: rivalry is merely shifted from being between individual schools to being between specified groupings of schools, e.g. between the state-maintained and independent sectors. But the offending shadow of unfettered competition is at least lifted.

Examples of Recent Group Marketing

There is evidence of growing interest in group or collaborative marketing. In Alderley Edge near Manchester, for example, a number of maintained sector schools have undertaken group marketing to counteract pro-active marketing by local independent schools. And in Bristol, as described elsewhere, numerous schools there have recently organized a joint PR programme. Though a few other illustrations of group marketing can be found, it is the USA that provides a more enlightening vantage point from which to observe this phenomenon in action. There, as many as 30 group or collaborative marketing strategies had been identified in 1987 in the boarding-school sector alone.[1] In the state of Maine, nine schools recently established a highly successful group marketing campaign. And 29 schools in Minneapolis–St Paul established the Twin Cities Admission Association, which involved, among other things, a highly successful joint Schools Fair at the leading exhibition, Expo' 86 – so successful, in fact, that the Twin Cities Admission Association now gains wide television coverage of their collaborative marketing activities.

These examples attest to the considerable advantages of group or collaborative marketing which are that it

- distributes costs among participating schools
- helps professional development through exchange of ideas and marketing experience
- assists the public to more easily identify a single source from which to obtain information on all participating schools
- establishes formidable lobby of participating schools
- provides greater chance of attracting media coverage since joint activities look less like explicit advertising and appeal to a wider audience
- enhances public image of participating schools

Practical Activities for Group Marketing

Collaborative activities might include: commissioning special market research studies, coordinating product decisions, undertaking joint corporate publicity and advertising, organizing joint open days, exhibitions and education fairs, pooling of resources, expertise and experiences relevant to marketing, sharing cost of producing prospectuses, directories, direct mail and other publicity and advertising materials, forming marketing agencies.

Key points

1 In some circumstances, group or collaborative marketing helps to resolve the moral dilemma facing those schools who are hesitant about marketing.
2 Group or collaborative marketing involves a number of schools with shared interests and values who would ordinarily compete with each other in the same market.
3 Though more evident in the USA, there is growing interest in group or collaborative marketing among British schools.
4 The advantages of group or collaborative marketing are considerable.

Notes

1 See Boarding Schools, *The New Marketing Handbook for Independent Schools*, Boarding School, Boston, MA, 1987.

7

Defining Education Products

In recent years there has been much analysis of what makes a good school. The one consistent finding is that strong leadership is essential. A head able to lead from the front and enthuse his or her staff will be rewarded by teachers determined to make a success of their jobs. When choosing a school, spend a lot of time talking to the head. And do your best to find out what teachers and pupils think of him or her. It could tell you a lot more than a list of examination results.[1]

Introduction

Faced with the threat of closure, Simon Digby Secondary School in Chelmsley Wood, Solihull, set about 'selling' its product to local decision-makers as part of a concerted campaign to reverse the LEA's proposal. But what exactly was Simon Digby selling? Unlike manufactured goods, educational products are not things. So, local politicians were invited to the school to experience first-hand the nature, content and quality of its offering.[2] And nearby, Churchfields High School adopted a similar strategy, though for different reasons, as its head, Edwin Smith, explains:

> I have made a positive effort to get the school seen as it really is, by having adults in the lessons and parents assembly. The quality of the teaching has always been first-class, and pupils' behaviour is good in a non-repressive regime – yet, until recently, people were never welcomed into the school buildings to see any of this.[3]

Evidently, educational products cannot be 'sold' through conventional channels of distribution; they lack concrete attributes which make this possible. Herein lies the marketing challenge for schools: to make known or convey to parents and prospective pupils the features of the service they offer them. Understanding the nature of the education product is essential in deciding realistic marketing communication strategies.

Features of the Education Product

In essence, education is 'a process or a series of processes performed for the benefit of a consumer (the pupil)',[4] not a concrete entity. More specifically, it is a service and as such manifests a number of characteristics which clearly distinquish it from non-service products.

First, education is essentially intangible: it cannot be stored or acquired in any material sense, nor can ownership of education be conferred on the consumer (the pupil) or customer (parent). Education products are essentially ephemeral.

Second, a product feature of education is its human dimension. From a consumer/customer perspective, education is inextricably linked to those responsible for delivering the service: teachers and support staff, whose skills, enthusiasm, commitment and personality form an integral part of the product.

A third feature is trust. Given education's ephemeral nature, consumers and customers cannot know what will be received until the service is rendered (though the school's reputation may give them a fair idea). Education services can only be described, they cannot be measured or physically examined prior to purchase. Consumers and customers therefore seek to acquire education services on the expectation that it will provide a specified benefit or benefits.

Fourth, education manifests a number of material attributes. Though the education product is essentially ephemeral, it includes a number of tangible features also: physical buildings in which learning takes place, libraries, books, special study packs, sport facilities, language and science laboratories, and so on.

Finally, the education product is comprised of both core and non-core elements.[5] The former refers to those aspects of the service which are central to it: basic intrinsic features of education that represent the largely intangible benefits and fundamental requirements which consumer (pupil) and customer (parent) perceive the service offers them. Essentially, these attributes are based on the pupil's/parent's subjective, personal assessment of what it is they believe an education product provides. For example: experience; opportunity; feeling of achievement; self-realization; increased self-esteem; confidence; enjoyment. By contrast, non-core elements are principally extrinsic tangible entities, and comprise the 'packaging' of intrinsic features; the latter cannot exist independently of the former: formal teaching activities (intrinsic/ephemeral element), for example, takes place in the classroom (extrinsic/tangible, package element).

Using the continua intangible/tangible and intrinsic/extrinsic, the matrix in figure 7.1 categorizes the various constituents of education.

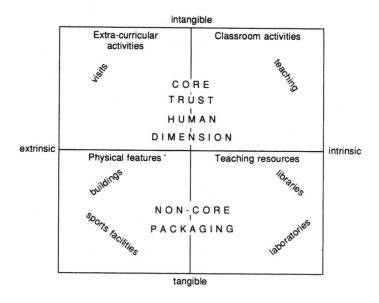

Figure 7.1 Constituents of the education product

Relevance of Product Features to Marketing Schools

Almost invariably, a key marketing strategy for schools involves conveying the attributes of their respective products to pupils and parents. The nature of education, however, poses special problems here. While conventional methods of media advertising are suitable for communicating the tangible features of education (physical features and teaching resources in figure 7.1), it is singularly inappropriate for conveying the ephemeral: teaching and extra-curricular activities are simply too abstract for advertising in this way since 'most media are already one step removed from reality their abstracting capabilities often make [the] service . . . more hazy instead of more concrete'.[6]

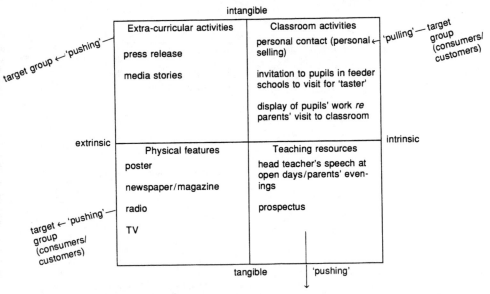

Figure 7.2 Education product characteristics: impact on advertising and communication activities

Evidently, the answer lies in the school working hard at making the attributes or selling points it wishes to convey to consumers and customers, seem real by building a case from tangible evidence.[7] In other words, the school must select a means of communication which is suitable for the purpose. Figure 7.2 offers guidance here. Where a school's selling points are essentially intangible, i.e. fall into the 'extra-curricular' and 'classroom activities' categories, then direct contact or personal selling, rather than media exposure, is the more apt means of communicating product characteristics to prospective pupils and parents. Indeed, product elements 'trust' and 'human dimension' (see figure 7.1) cannot be expressed in any other way. Here, direct contact between consumer/customer and school staff is vital: only by talking to teachers, sampling teaching and learning methods and perusing exhibits of pupils' work, will consumers and customers gain insight into the quality and attitudes of staff and appreciate the intangible and intrinsic elements in the school's offering. In this way, a school is able to introduce tangible evidence into its communication activities. By contrast, non-core, packaging features are sufficiently concrete to allow the use of conventional advertising and related media.

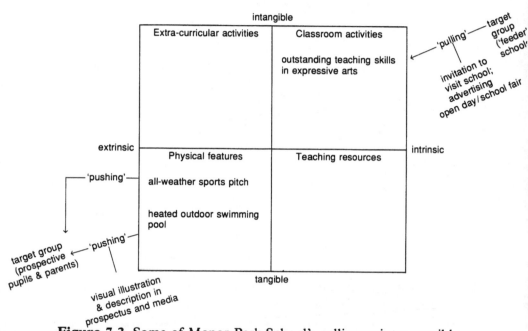

Figure 7.3 Some of Manor Park School's selling points: possible communication activities

To demonstrate the application of this approach to a real-life situation, a special study has been undertaken of the product range offered by Manor Park Secondary School in Nuneaton, Warwickshire. Much of Manor Park's offering is similar to that of its competitors'. But some aspects of the school's product do stand out as different: 'outstanding teaching skills in expressive arts', 'heated outdoor swimming pool' and 'all-weather sports pitch'. How might these attributes, then, be communicated to consumers? Reflecting the various product characteristics of Manor

Park's products, figure 7.3 illustrates possible communication strategies. (Many of the techniques identified here are described in detail in chapter 10).

Identifying the School's Selling Points

Most schools tend to offer much the same product to consumers and customers; one head estimates that about 85 per cent of all educational offerings are indistinguishable.[8] The school's marketing decision-makers must therefore identify, develop and promote one or more selling points, i.e. product features or attributes which distinquish the institution from its competitors. In undertaking this activity, a systematic and integrated approach must be adopted and full account taken of the school's corporate mission and objectives.

Generally, a school's selling points find expression or shape in tangible, extrinsic, non-core, packaging product elements; seldom are they ephemeral, core aspects of education. Every education service has descriptive technical features which can differentiate it from competing institutions.[9] A survey of school advertisments which have recently appeared in the media provides an abundance of descriptive phrases to support this observation.

- wide range of sporting and cultural activities
- heated outdoor swimming pool
- extensive playing fields
- all-weather tennis courts
- computers
- small classes
- many extra-curricular activities

- school situated in 6 acres of woodland
- school located in spacious grounds
- school located in beautiful and historic setting

- visits and foreign exchanges
- traditional education
- broad education
- quality education
- excellent examination results
- individual attention
- excellent general education

Table 7.1   Three magnet schools distinguished by timetables

Timetable One: Technology and Technology of the Arts magnet.

Period	Monday	Tuesday	Wednesday	Thursday	Friday
1/2	English	Technology	History	Top-up*	French
3/4	Science	RE	Maths	Geography	Magnet B*
5/6	Art/Music	Science	Science	Magnet A*	PE/Games
7/8	Maths	Magnet A*	Magnet B*	English	Science

* Magnet A: Choice of computer studies, electronics, media/film studies, engineering science, art and design, second modern language.
* Magnet B: Choice of graphics, motor vehicle studies, computer studies, business/information studies, art and design, second modern language.

Timetable Two: Leisure, Sports, Travel and Tourism magnet.

Period	Monday	Tuesday	Wednesday	Thursday	Friday
1/2	English	Technology	Science	Maths	Science
3/4	French	Science	RE	English	Magnet A*
5/6	Art/Music	History	Magnet A*	Science	Geography
7/8	Maths	Top-up*	Magnet B*	Magnet B*	PE/Games

* Magnet A: Choice of business and information studies or Spanish.
* Magnet B: Choice of outdoor education or travel and tourism.

Timetable Three: Any magnet school.

Period	Monday	Tuesday	Wednesday	Thursday	Friday
1/2	English	History	Technology	Science	Computer Studies*
3/4	Science	RE	Maths	English	French
5/6	Art/Music	Science	German*	Geography	Science
7/8	Maths	Computer Studies*	Top-up*	German*	PE/Games

Above are three examples of timetables that might be followed by 14- to 16-year-olds in magnet schools. 30 out of 40 35-minute periods a week (or 15 out of 20 double periods) are occupied by national curriculum subjects, on the assumption that a pupil is following a full science course, occupying 20 per cent of the timetable. The remaining 10 periods (five double periods) are devoted to options, which are asterisked in the examples. The first two timetables show how pupils in two different magnet schools might spend their week. The third timetable is an example of a standard one that would be available to any pupil in any school. Optional subjects such as computer studies and German could be taken, even though they might have no relevance to the school's magnet specialism.

In all three timetables, one double period is reserved for a 'top-up' option, enabling the pupil to take a full GCSE course in history, geography, technology, French or creative arts, all of which must be studied for at least two periods in the national curriculum

Source: *Independent*, 24 August 1989.

- school with a secure future
- longer school day
- specialist teaching in performing arts
- technological education
- guarantee of place in senior school/post 16 education

In order to attain relative uniqueness in product offering, and in consequence secure a better competitive position, two practical techniques are available to schools: differentiation and branding.

Product differentiation

Special features and packaging of educational services are designed to add value or quality to the intrinsic education product. By creating value-added selling points, a school can expect its product to stand out from those offered by competitors. This activity is called product differentiation.

By developing a differentiated product, a school is able to establish a relatively unique place in the education market. In this way, the product becomes closely associated with the school in the consumers' mind and it becomes increasingly difficult for competitors to imitate the product. To this extent, differentiation is a competitive device and offers a means of market protection.

Creating a distinct education product is not easy,[10] but many schools have had considerable success recently in introducing product differentiation into education provision. The formal establishment in Birmingham of a pre-school Montessori playgroup, which takes children at 2.5 years of age, is one example. And magnet schools in New York is another. They have created a differentiated product which is targeted at a specified market segment, i.e. those consumers and customers in New York who seek a specialized curriculum. Table 7.1 illustrates three possible magnet schools based on differing curricula.

Branding

This is a technique for identifying a product by a registered name or distinctive trade mark. As with product differentiation, it is closely associated with adding value and quality to education services.

Given the ephemeral nature of services generally, branding is important to all service products such as education because it provides much-needed consistency and credibility. Moreover, the technique, because of its capacity to represent the synthesis of multiple qualities or claims in a single name, 'offers the service sector a marketing tool of unparalleled potential'.[11] More specifically, branding performs an invaluable role for school marketing: it contributes to the promotion of education products, and it helps fend off competition by offering a 'unique and protectable aura'[12] which it can build for an intangible service.

Key points

1 Understanding the nature of the education product is essential in deciding realistic marketing communication strategies.
2 An education product is comprised of a number of features:

- intangibility
- human dimension
- trust
- material attributes
- core or intrinsic constituents and non-core, extrinsic 'packaging' elements

3 Conventional methods of media advertising are suitable for communicating the tangible features of education, but not its ephemeral elements; the latter is better conveyed by direct contact with prospective pupils and parents, i.e. personal selling.
4 Since most schools tend to offer much the same product to consumers and customers, it is important to strive to identify, develop and promote one or more selling points.
5 A school's product can gain a competitive edge by

- differentiation
- branding

Notes

1 Barry Hugill, *Observer*, 13 October 1991.
2 Though highly favourable were the impressions gleaned from their visit to Simon Digby, LEA decision-makers were unable

to reverse their decision to close the school on the grounds of falling rolls. The school closed September, 1992.

3 Anna Foster, 'Comprehensive Solution', *Management Today*, August, 1989.
4 M. MacDonald and J. W. Leppard, *How To Sell A Service*, Heinemann, London, 1988, p. 125.
5 G. Lynn Shostack, 'A Framework for Service Marketing', in S. W. Brown and R. P. Fisk, *Marketing Theory*, John Wiley & Sons Inc, New York, 1984, p. 250.
6 Ibid. p. 257.
7 Ibid. p. 255.
8 In interview, head master, Manor Park School, Nuneaton, December 1989.
9 MacDonald and Leppard, *How to Sell*.
10 R. Taylor, 'The Branding of a Service', in J. M. Murphy (ed.), *Branding: a Key Marketing Tool*, Macmillan, London, 1987, p. 125.
11 Ibid. p. 128.
12 Ibid.

8

Image-building

When I came for my interview and looked around I noticed one thing. The students said "hello" when I spoke to them. That told me a great deal about the place. I took to it straight away. I saw a good school that was being misjudged and had a poor reputation.[1]

Introduction

It is incontestable that parents and prospective pupils are inordinately influenced in their choice of school by consideration of reputation or image. Their perceptions in this matter, well founded or otherwise, form a basis or reality by which they discriminate between rival institutions. For this reason, corporate image-building is usually central to a school's marketing strategy.

In the context of marketing, a school's image is 'the net result of the interaction of all experiences, impressions, beliefs, feelings and knowledge people have about [it]'[2] and involves reinforcing positive messages about the institution itself, not its curricula and educational facilities.

Benefits of a Good Corporate Image

By creating an effective corporate image, a school is better placed to influence public perception of it in terms which are more positive, powerful and favourable. More specifically, a school will gain increased:

- parent/pupil/community awareness of it – and in consequence, is likely to be viewed more favourably by client groups and external audience[3]
- effectiveness in internal and external communication – it will provide a common, visual format for all messages, thus offering a critical degree of consistency
- involvement of staff in the marketing process – teachers are more likely to relate to school's ethos and feel less alienated from it (possibly resulting in fewer resignations, increased commitment and a sense of *esprit de corps*), and may be better motivated to act as ambassadors to promote the school

Measuring Image

A prerequisite to corporate image-building involves gauging clients' current perceptions of the school relative to its main competitors'. In undertaking this task, answers to a number of key questions must be sought:

- What sort of image do parents, prospective pupils, public and others, have of the school?
- How do they see it in comparison to its main competitors?
- Do they view it in favourable or unfavourable terms?
- What do those market segments whom the school wishes to attract, think of it?

In short, a school needs to measure its image. Several methods are available for accomplishing this objective, two of which are familiarity – favourability analysis and image profiling. These are discussed in Appendix D.

Image-building

A number of complementary techniques and activities exist to help schools promote a consistent and effective visual and corporate identity. These comprise public relations, logos and symbols, signage, prospectuses, stationery, and attitudinal and behavioural features of key front-line staff, head teacher, teachers, pupils and support personnel. Most of these elements are outlined here, others are covered in subsequent chapters.

A good visual image is one that affords its owner easy and favourable recognition. It also reflects the school's corporate objectives and strategy and makes explicit its organizational personality. Essentially, an effective visual image is

- memorable
- unique
- appropriate

Logo

This is the most appropriate and easily understood visual sign for building a school's corporate identity. Indeed, many schools consider the logo or symbol to be the an important image-building tool (Appendix A, survey results, question 16).

The logo takes one of three forms: symbol (see exhibit 8.1), monogram or logotype.[4]

BIRCHWOOD COMMUNITY HIGH SCHOOL

Exhibit 8.1 Birchwood Community High School logo

Characteristics of an effective logo

Based on Keen's study,[5] an effective school logo will manifest five characteristics:

Distinctiveness: An effective logo stands apart from those of its competitors. In this sense, it provides a form of 'branding' which helps to distinquish it from other schools.

Obvious and meaningful association with the school: The logo must relate to and be readily identifiable with the school. This can be achieved where it reflects or encapsulates an easily recognized aspect or feature of the school.

Compatibility with the school's PR strategy: In this context, the successful logo should underpin and complement the school's PR strategy.

For example, if it is intended to convey an image of a 'caring, approachable and friendly school', then the logo must reflect this with, for example, a less formal design – a logotype based on hand-written script may achieve the desired effect.

Simplicity: The less complex the logo, the easier it is to use and the greater its adaptability.

Attractiveness: It seems self-evident that consumers generally are likely to feel more disposed towards an organization whose logo is appealing. In the context of education, the adoption of an attractive logo may also help to encourage staff to feel part of the school.

A recently designed logo for South East Essex College of Arts and Technology, successfully incorporates all the above features (exhibit 8.2). This highly appealing and apposite visual design offers the college an effective corporate identity.

Exhibit 8.2 South East Essex College of Arts and Technology logo

Assessing the effectiveness of a new school logo

If a school's logo fulfills all the above criteria, it will prove a vital asset to the creation of a corporate identity. Ultimately, however, the effectiveness of any logo must be determined by marketing research: it will be necessary to ascertain how distinctive, meaningful, attractive and effective, consumers actually find it to be. This assessment can be conducted simply by reproducing the logo in the format it is intended to take, and, using a structured questionnaire, gauging staff, pupil and public reaction to it. Alternatively, a school may choose to engage a firm of market researchers, such as the UK company Scantel, to test for effectiveness and impact.

Tools for Image-building

An effective school logo, then, is a powerful marketing tool for creating a visual corporate identity. But the logo must, as far as practicable, be used in a uniform manner and applied consistently to all outward expressions of the school's existence: letter heads, school uniforms, school vehicles, display signs and boards, etc. In this context, special consideration should be given to the prospectus, signage, stationery and other physical manifestations of the school's corporate identity.

School prospectus

The prospectus is considered an important element in image building (Appendix A, survey results, question 16). In this context, it performs a number of key functions:

- it can be used to make a powerful statement about a school's philosophy and curriculum
- it performs a number of promotion functions, such as advertising and PR, and complements other image-building and communication activities
- it is, for some pupils/students, their main source of information about curricula and courses

The task of a prospectus is to state what the school stands for, where it is going and why it is worth becoming a pupil there. But if a prospectus is to be truly effective, it must convey these interconnected messages to its intended audience with accuracy and sensitivity: in promoting schools, the hard sell does not work.

The design aspects of a prospectus must be undertaken with due care and full consideration given to all relevant marketing objectives and strategies. A mere cosmetic adjustment to an existing prospectus is unlikely to prove helpful to image-building.

In constructing a prospectus, special consideration must be given to cover and content.

Cover This feature of a prospectus is of critical importance to effective image building: it forms the reader's first impression of the school. The cover must be composed in such a way that maximum impact is attained. To achieve this, the cover of the prospectus must:

- stand out as different from other school prospectuses
- be visually attractive, sufficiently to make the enquirer want to read its content
- relate to the reader, i.e. be clear in meaning and easily understood
- introduce the reader to the school, its philosophy and product, i.e. convey the right image
- contain an appropriate balance of visual material: not too much detail but enough to make a clear statement of purpose
- clearly display relevant symbols of school's corporate identity, i.e. its logo

It is noticeable that few school prospectuses adhere to all or even most of the above prescriptions. Observe, for example, how many contain photographic illustrations of school buildings. In some instances, it may be appropriate to do this; for example, where specified buildings represent part of a school's identity. But does it, on the whole, help a school's prospectus stand out from those of its competitors? All schools have buildings.

The Louisville Collegiate School's prospectus illustrates the point. The school's former prospectus consisted of a photograph of the entrance to the main building. This was replaced by a more appealing photograph of two students, one male one female, both neatly dressed, carrying books and papers, and, most importantly, smiling into the camera. The photograph conveys important information about the school, such as:

- that it is coeducational
- that academic study is important
- that structure and order are important (as conveyed by smart dress)
- that pupils are happy there
- that the head-on posture seeks to engage the reader with a sense of forthrightness

Content Though the cover of the prospectus performs a key role in building the school's image, its content also contributes to this process. Principally, the prospectus content helps to sell the school's product by advertising and highlighting its attributes. But it clearly impacts on the reader's perception of the institution, too. It therefore contributes to image-building. The material must inform readers of all they want and need to know about the school, and give parents and pupils an idea of what they will be doing at the school and the nature of their involvement. In effect, it amplifies and qualifies the image communicated by the cover. The type of information and level of detail required will depend on the school; for example, boarding schools need to describe activities outside formal teaching sessions.

Research has shown that the salient features of an effective education prospectus are, among other things:

A clear and comprehensive statement of all relevant information Consumers want and need to know about such matters as: statement of school philosophy; approaches to teaching and learning; student/pupil support and counselling services; education programme; class sizes; extra-curricular activities; recreational and sports facilities; procedures for admission (if relevant); residential life (if boarding school); religious life; health services; accommodation; assessment; prizes; achievements by pupils; and so on.

Pupils' comments on the school This has been described by Northfield Mount Hermon School in the USA as 'unobstructive views'.

Case studies These are profiles of alumni and their career achievements since leaving school.

Material that is written with the reader's interests and motives in mind.

Signage

This is another important aspect of visual image-building that performs a major PR function. Effective signposting will help schools to modify their image quickly without undue expense.[6] Moreover, it is also another means of showing visitors what the school has to offer by way of recreational and sports facilities. Signposts should pin-point and highlight a school's special physical features (its packaging): 'To heated swimming pool', 'To all-weather tennis courts', and so on. It is worth nothing that, in this context, an acceptable, non-aggressive, non-competitive and ethical form of advertising can take place.

To take advantage of the image-building and advertising functions offered here, the school's layout and signage must be planned from the perspective of the visitor. Are signposts unambiguous and easily understood by visitors? Is adequate attention paid to visitors whose first language is not English? Does existing signage clearly indicate the location of the school's entrance hall and main buildings? Does existing signposting clearly identify (advertise!) the school's best physical features?

Clearly, apt signposting stimulates visitors into forming favourable impressions of a school. Information conveyed in this way makes a powerful statement about an institution.

Stationery and other forms of image-building

Stationery embossed with the school's logo provides an opportunity for promoting corporate identity since it is an important point of contact between staff/pupils and parents and public. Letter headings can be especially effective in this respect (see exhibit 8.3). Similarly, other features of schools help build a corporate image by promoting visual identity, such as strap-lines on school brochures, distinctive school uniforms, and livery on school mini-bus.

Attitudinal and Behavioural Aspects of Image-building: Front-line Staff/pupils/support personnel

Another key component of a successful PR package for schools, is responsive front-line staff: those members of the school community with whom parents, prospective pupils, governors and the public most frequently come into contact. In this context, front-line staff include head teacher, deputy head teachers, senior pupils responsible for supervising visitors, receptionists, telephonists and staff available to talk with parents at open day/evenings.

In many instances, success or failure of a school's image-building and PR campaign is largely determined by front-line pupils/staff, for it is they who present the institution's public face. 'Much of the effort that has gone into creating a caring, responsive image', Green argues, 'will be destroyed if there is dissonance between the perception of those with whom we do business that we work so hard to create and the reality of our follow-through'.[7] But the marketing process permeates the whole of an organization,

Junior Headteacher:

Mr. D. J. Halford
B.A., M.Ed., A.C.P.,
Adv. Dip. Ed.

Tel: 061-633 1693

Infant/Nursery Headteacher

Mrs. J. A. Mackie
Adv. Dip. Ed.

Tel: 061-624 3593

THE RICHMOND SCHOOLS

Together we learn

Address: Winterbottom Street
OLDHAM
Lancashire
OL9 6HY.

When replying, please address correspondence to _____

Oldham Metropolitan Borough

Exhibit 8.3 The Richmond Schools' letter head

and the efforts by front-line staff must be fully supported and complemented by circumspect behaviour on the part of all pupils and others representing the school.

Head teacher

Clearly, the qualities, attitudes and behaviour of those responsible for leading a school will impact on others' perception of the institution and their feelings towards it. But what characteristics are both befitting of a school's head and commensurate with the promotion of a good corporate image as well?

A recent survey of 1,500 senior managers found that the most needed quality for a chief executive was a strong sense of vision: a quality not of 'drawing imaginary pictures about the future . . . (but) having an intimate knowledge of the organisation, of the market in which it is operating and of the interfaces between these two elements'.[8]

In the context of schools, at least two other qualities are associated with strong leadership: established public profile and ability to make apt speeches/presentations on open days and similar public occasions.[9] Material in chapter 9 deals with the former. In the latter case, a good speech is likely to cover sequentially the following points:

- statement affirming the school's values (for example, 'fair and caring institution')
- comments reinforcing the school's high standards in pupils' behaviour and their positive attitudes, and other relevant achievements (good academic results, for example)
- reference to possible progression routes, for example, sixth form study, if relevant, giving examples of successes, both in terms of examination results, higher education places gained and careers pursued
- statement about the school's position in market place
- if applicable, reference to demand for places, for example, length of the waiting list for entry to the school
- reinforce message about the school's position in market place

Pupils

Often, a school's Head Teacher is the most obvious promoter of its public face. But considerable impact on consumers' perception of a school is also exercised by receptionists and senior pupils responsible for supervising visitors.

Senior pupils are especially important in this respect because they present, in effect, the 'end-product' of the school's educational service. Though obvious, it is a point worth reiterating: parents considering the school for their offspring cannot avoid making impressionistic judgements based on their perception of senior pupils. They may think: 'That's how my son (or daughter) will be when he (or she) reaches lower sixth.' A senior pupil who presents a poor image, appears flippant, discourteous, uninterested, for example, may put off such parents. Senior pupils must therefore project a confident, polite, mature and responsible manner. For most schools, this will not present a problem: generally, most senior pupils fall into the latter category. Indeed, pupils are often a school's best PR agent.

Receptionists and telephonists

Another key aspect of a school's public face is the visitors' reception area. This is important to a school's success in image-building, for, as Colin Kennedy points out, 'a courteous and attentive receptionist will do more good than any amount of signposting'.[10]

In most schools, administrative staff undertake this important task. But pupils can play an important part here. Sitting behind a reception desk, senior pupils can be ready to welcome and direct visitors to their destination. In order to minimize the distraction from formal study, and distribute equitably the responsibility and time commitment, a rota system is used. Pupils themselves clearly benefit from this involvement: it is a position of responsibility and encourages their direct participation in promoting the school. A number of maintained sector schools such as Henley-in-Arden High and Manor Park have successful involved pupils in this process.

Telephone contact between school and parent constitutes a further manifestation of a school's public face, a point which is discussed further in the next chapter. And its importance is incontestable: 'the majority of practical day-to-day communications', Green stresses, 'takes place over the telephone. In many cases, its the first point-of-contact that many people have with our organisations.'[11]

Here, a school's secretary, senior staff or trained telephonist undertake this vital communication task. While special training for this activity is available, simple common sense rules of conduct will suffice. Indeed, the skill needed to implement this task effectively belies its importance: 'the perception of a good service rather than explicit action is what really makes an impact. The fact that somebody sounds interested in what's being said and is sympathetic to their real or imaginary problems is what's important.'[12]

Managing the Corporate Image

The possession of a good visual and corporate image is a prized asset for any educational establishment. It has been estimated that enhancing or building-up a school's image takes five to ten years depending on how well known it is, but its deterioration can be a rapid concomitant of even a short burst of adverse publicity.[13]

If the effectiveness of a corporate image is to be sustained, it must be carefully and tightly managed, and nurtured from the top. In other words, the various activities involved in building a school's image must be initiated, planned, coordinated, controlled and monitored, and throughout, a uniformity of visual expression and corporate attitude and behaviour maintained. In this process, a school's senior staff must assume direct responsibility for managing this aspect of PR. In exercising responsibility, senior staff must deploy appropriate strategies that actively encourage the involvement of the school community in supporting and promoting the school's corporate image. To realize this objective, it is essential that senior staff maintain constant communication with four key audiences: pupils, subordinate staff, parents and public.

Key points

1 An effective corporate image will help a school achieve a positive, powerful and favourable image.
2 It is vital that a school first measures its image to ascertain how others see it.
3 There are two especially useful methods for image measurement:

- familiarity – favourability analysis
- image profiling

4 A school's image can be enhanced by building a suitable visual and corporate identity.
5 One of the most useful mechanisms for creating a visual identity is the logo.
6 To be truly effective, the logo must be

- distinctive
- meaningful
- compatible with the PR strategy

- simple
- attractive

7 Tools for image-building include

- school prospectus
- signage
- stationery

8 Front-line personnel are also key to successful corporate image building, especially

- head teacher
- pupils
- receptionists & telephonists

9 The corporate image must be very carefully managed throughout.

Notes

1 Recollection of a recently appointed head teacher, in Anna Foster, 'Comprehensive Solution', *Management Today*, August, 1989.

2 Stewart Lewis, 'Building and Measuring the Image', Paper presented to Conference *Communicating A Corporate Image*, London, 12/10/1988. A similar definition is offered by Topor who describes 'image' as the '. . . . aggregate, or sum, of feelings, beliefs, attitudes, impressions, thoughts, perceptions, ideas, recollections, conclusions, and mind sets someone has about an institution, its components, or its products'. See Robert S. Topor, *Institutional Image: How to Define, Improve, Market it*, Washington, DC: Council for Advancement and Support of Education, 1986.

3 Stewart Lewis, 'Building and Measuring'. Here Lewis argues: 'Familiarity breeds favourability, not contempt. Nine times out of ten, and among every public we've studies and in every country we've done research – 28 at the last count – we've found a high correlation between how well people know a company and how highly they regard it. The higher the regard, the higher the public' propensity to buy products or shares, apply for a job or recommended products to others, and to listen to the company's point of view on controversial issues'.

4 C. Keen et al., (eds), *Visual and Corporate Identity*, HEIST Publications, Banbury, UK, 1989.

5 Ibid.

6 Ibid., pp. 107, 109

7 G. Green, 'The Importance of Telephone Contact', Paper presented to Conference Communicating A Corporate Image, London, 12 October 1988.

8 Andrew Kakabadse, 'A Listening Boss Makes the Vision Work', *The Sunday Times*, 29 October 1989.

9 Phillip Laycock and Malcolm Watson, 'Analysis, Marketing and Communications', paper presented to HEIST Conference The Entrepreneurial School, Birmingham Polytechnic, UK 1/7/91.

10 Colin Kennedy, 'Signage – A second View', in Keen et al., *Visual and Corporate Identity*, p. 110.

11 G. Green, 'The Importance of Telephone Contact'.

12 Ibid.

13 Boarding Schools, *The New Marketing Handbook for Independent Schools* (pamphlet), Boarding Schools, Boston, 1987, p. 9

9

Public Relations

Public relations (PR) is a 'deliberate, planned and sustained effort to establish and maintain mutual understanding between an organisation and its public',[1] and involves the 'execution of a campaign to place favourable information in newspapers or other media at minimal or no financial cost'.[2] In another sense, it is about the projection of a school's corporate image.[3] Essentially, PR involves informing parents, community and others about the school itself, not its products. In contrast to advertising, which consists of directing a single message at a specified target segment,[4] PR is concerned with communicating many interconnected messages to a larger, unspecified audience.

Value of PR to Schools

PR contributes to the marketing effort in a number of particulars. First, it helps a school raise its public profile. In this respect, PR is more effective than advertising.[5] But it cannot disguise a school's shortcomings: 'if the public portrayal of an organization is merely a facade to conceal undesirable behaviour', Kincaid warns, 'the public relations program is doomed to failure from the start'.[6] Second, PR is, relative to other promotion activities such as advertising, financially affordable to all schools: technically, it is 'free'. Third, PR enables a school to publicize its corporate identity which helps staff feel less alienated from the institution, thereby enhancing their commitment to it. Fourth, it provides, over time, a means of changing peoples' perception of the school. Here, it facilitates the adoption of pro-active rather than reactive strategies, thus enabling the school to pre-empt events/situations that might adversely affect its desired image, i.e. the way it wishes others to see it. This might include explaining the context of examination results, or fostering positive views about the school's endeavours. Fifth, PR is by the teaching profession's standards ethical, since it promotes the school without denigrating rival educational institutions. Finally, by presenting a consistent message to internal and external audiences, PR offers them both continual reassurance about the purposefulness of the school and the attractiveness of being associated with it.

Sources of Expertise

While the resource implications for most PR activities is virtually insignificant, some dexterity is usually required to implement them. For most schools, this is unlikely to present major problems: educational institutions often possess a number of staff members who have a flair for publicity, ability to construct press releases, or other communication skills relevant to PR work. Where this is not possible, then the services of an independent agency or PR consultant might be sought. For many schools, this is prohibitively expensive. But, where this is feasible, then placing responsibility for all PR activities with one, reputable PR agency or consultant specializing in education, may prove judicious: generally, the success of a promotion campaign is sustainable only if PR is reinforced and underpinned by other constituents of the communication mix, such as advertising and personal selling. A single PR agency or consultant is better placed to ensure that all activities in the mix are effectively coordinated and form part of a coherent plan.

Prerequisites for PR

The success of a school's PR programme – which usually becomes apparent from 6 to 12 months after its inception – is dependent on

- careful planning
- participation of all staff and pupils
- commitment of all staff and pupils to the objectives of the PR programme

- all staff and pupils being aware of the PR programme and appreciative of their roles
- compatibility with prevailing educational values and mores

PR Activities for Schools

PR involves any activity concerned with the projection of a school's corporate identity. For practical purposes, this includes:

- press releases
- press receptions
- media stories and feature articles
- exhibitions of pupils' work
- schools' trade fair
- telephone

Press release

This involves producing copy which an editor of local, regional or, exceptionally, national newspaper can use as[6] 'filler'. If adequate resources are available, then an outside agency can be employed to prepare and distribute copy to relevant editors. Most schools, however, are not so fortunately placed, and must undertake press release work themselves; below is given a brief exposition of best practice and guidelines for preparing a press release.

Most of the copy submitted by schools to editors is not published. A principal reason for rejection is failure on the part of the writer to appreciate what editors require. How, then, might a school construct a successful press release?

Your copy must provide editors with all they need to know about the school, what the point of the story is, where it will take place and when. In other words, good copy should adhere to the four *W*s by informing editors:

who you are
what your story is about
where it is located
when it is likely to happen

To construct good copy and enhance the likelihood of publication, special attention is needed when approaching editors, writing the press release, presenting the finished product to editors, and designing illustrative material. Consideration should be given also to the possible advantages of using press receptions to promote your school.

Approaching editors In undertaking this initial step in placing the school's press release, there are a number of considerations to bear in mind:

- Provide editors with the opportunity to write an exclusive about a newsworthy story associated with your school.
- Know publication deadlines and best days for submission. Editors are more receptive to new stories the day after press day – the 'dead days'. Know the dead days of the publication you are interested in.
- Research your story thoroughly.
- Ensure your story is appropriate for the publication.
- Be honest with editors.
- Develop working relationships with helpful journalists.
- Add a personal touch when writing to editors, i.e. address correspondence to them personally, ensuring their name is correctly spelled, and address envelope by hand rather than typed on – it helps differentiate it from most other correspondence an editor receives.
- Ensure staff member is easily attainable and always available for follow-up, even during school vacations. Give work and home telephone numbers, limiting the times when a staff member is free to speak to an editor is tantamount to telling him to call at your convenience, not his!
- Return calls from editors immediately.

Writing the press release Similarly, there are a number of points to be borne in mind when constructing the press release:

- Highlight the main point(s) of story at the beginning (ensure that the opening paragraph contains all the punch lines). Describe the story in concise and dramatic terms.
- Paragraphs should use sentences which are succinct and few in number.
- Avoid using superlatives and long-winded quotations.
- When writing for local or regional press, always use a local angle.
- A contact name, address and telephone number must be included on the release.
- Do not advertise or use a style of language or jargon associated with it.

- Do not make exaggerated claims or statements.
- Take account of the knowledge and educational level of the publication's average reader. It is a rule of thumb when writing for UK newspapers to assume you are writing for a knowledgeable 12-year-old who is capable of reading and understanding clearly written English. The UK's national newspaper, the *Daily Mail*, is pitched at this level; the UK's the *Sun* is aimed at reading age of about 7 years.
- Monitor closely any changes made by editors when the story is published. A better understanding of the newspaper's requirements for future reference can be gleaned from this process.

Presenting the press release   This is another key stage in maximizing the press release's appeal to editors. In this context, account should be taken of the following ten factors:

- Include one paragraph at the bottom of first page which summarizes the entire story and which can be used by itself, should the rest of the text be edited out.
- Keep it short. Length of copy must not exceed two sides of A4.
- Contents must be typed, preferably using double spacing and a two-inch left margin. This allows room for editing.
- Date of issue of copy must be clear to indicate freshness of story.
- The design and presentation of the copy must have impact on editors. The use of an effective logo at the top of the copy followed by the title 'News Release', will help achieve this.
- In some instances, a proviso may be necessary (for example 'Not for publication before 1 April 1990'). Otherwise, state 'for immediate release'. This information should be placed directly beneath copy heading.
- State number of words at top of copy.
- Highlight important points to make it stand out and differentiate it from stories submitted by other schools. But never underline as this is a printing instruction to set in italics.
- Number every page and include a continuation note at end of each page and top of the next.
- A relevant captioned photograph with the submitted copy will convey much information and will also appeal to editors.

Illustrative material   Illustrative material, such as relevant photographs, will increase appeal to editors. Photographs heighten interest and often convey more information than written narrative. When planning and constructing a press release, remember:

- Relevant photograph with the submitted copy will enhance the editor's interest. (It is important that any illustrative supporting material is captioned, with address and telephone number clearly written on it).
- Prints should be 8 × 6 inches and black and white.

Best practice: a recent example Implementation of the above guidelines, then, will help achieve press publication. Hitherto, many schools have successfully promoted their PR efforts by gaining media coverage in this way. Perhaps one of the most successful recent press releases is that produced by Henley-in-Arden High School in Warwickshire.

In order to publicize a sponsored parachute jump to help raise funds for extra facilities and resources, a press release was skilfully prepared by the school's Head Teacher.

PRESS RELEASE For immediate release

HENLEY GRANDFATHER IN SPONSORED PARACHUTE JUMP

Mr. Bill Mullings of High Street, Henley in Arden is planning a parachute jump for charity on Saturday 8th October. Mr. Mullings is the grandfather of a pupil at Henley High School. He is undertaking the jump to raise money for the Henley High School Association which provides extra facilities and resources for the School.

Henley High Headteacher – Mr. Ian Jackson – said

'I was both surprised and delighted when Mr. Mullings offered to take part in a sponsored event. We hope to buy a video camera for classroom use. Mr. Mullings originally offered to run a half marathon and then decided to add a parachute jump. We are very grateful for his energy and initiative.'

Mr. Mullings is a member of the High School Association Committee. He served in the 14th Army in Burma during World War Two and subsequently became a parachute jumping instructor in the R.A.F. He is a qualified teacher and worked for many years as an educational psychologist. Since his retirement he has been reading for an M.A. degree at the University of Keele.

Mr. Jackson commented.

'Mr. Mullings is a remarkable person. He tells me that he has over 100 parachute jumps to his credit and that he has run five marathons and several half marathons. There is therefore no shortage

Daredevil grandad

GRANDAD Bill Mullings is taking to the skies to raise cash for charity.

Bill, aged 66, is doing a sponsored parachute jump tomorrow to buy a £1,000 video camera for Henley High School, where his granddaughter Collette Waugh is a pupil.

The daredevil grandad, from Henley-in-Arden is no stranger to high-flying jumps – he was an RAF jumping instructor after serving with the 14th Army in Burma during the Second World War.

Superfit

But although he has more than 100 jumps under his belt, his last one was 25 years ago.

He said: 'I wouldn't say I'm apprehensive, but it will be an interesting experience to jump after all this time.'

Superfit Bill is also planning a half-marathon in November to add to the school funds.

The incredible grandad keeps his mind as fit as his body – by taking a part-time MA in psychology at Keele University.

He added: 'I may be retired, but I like to keep as active as possible, physically and mentally.'

Exhibit 9.1 *Stratford-on-Avon Evening Telegraph* front page feature

of expertise. This is a tremendous gesture and I hope that parents and friends of the School will support Mr. Mullings efforts in a generous manner.'

ENDS.

For further details contact Bill Mullings 05642–3151 and Ian Jackson 05642–2364

Many of the requirements for a successful press release are clearly seen in Henley-in-Arden School's copy. And this is reflected in the number of newspapers which carried the story: The *Stratford-on-Avon Evening Telegraph*, major front page feature; *Solihull News*, again, front page story; the *Observer* of Leamington Spa, and Solihull's *The Times*. Comparison between original copy and published stories reveal the extent to which editors developed the news release further, embellishing it with photographs in two instances. Such was the high quality and newsworthiness of Henley-in-Arden School's press release.

Press reception

As a general rule, most press receptions provide only limited opportunities for gaining news coverage of school events, though they are useful for counteracting adverse publicity where a school seeks to 'put its side of the story'. Where it is intended to use them, a number of points should be observed:

- Invitations should be distributed to relevant editors by personalized letter. The letter of invitation must attempt to sell the reception to editors: tell them *why* they should attend and *what* they will learn from it. Enclosed should be stamped addressed envelope, map of venue with all information on parking, and so on. Telephone editors the day before the event to remind them.
- Do not hold your reception when another competing event in the locality is taking place. And take account of local newspapers' deadlines when planning your conference.
- Persuade leading personalities to speak at the reception.
- Ensure venue looks packed. By selecting a venue which is small with insufficient chairs the desired effect can be created.
- Select venue which is easily accessible.
- Keep presentation short, allowing opportunity for questions.
- Be well prepared for questions.

Media stories and feature articles

Another worthwhile and financially free PR activity is media coverage of events associated with school. In contrast to press releases,
which necessarily deal with items of news, this activity deals with
stories about school and pupils which are of interest generally to
audiences. Media stories/features articles are usually designed for
a specific medium, such as press or television. Properly managed,
this form of publicity is extremely effective in promoting PR.

Most schools probably underestimate the media potential of
much of what they do. Pupils' achievements in examinations,
sports and creative arts, special school events, speech days, staff/
parent football and cricket matches, pupils' unusual hobbies and
pastimes, career achievements of alumni, and so on, are of potential interest to media editors.

A school's public relations officer must, therefore, develop appropriate techniques to tease-out relevant stories from staff and
pupils, secure publication of materials, and carefully manage the
publicity that accrues from them.

Generating stories   There are a number of tried and tested methods
for generating media stories and material for feature articles about a
school and its community. The publicity officer must endeavour to
closely involve all staff and pupils in this process; after all, it's their
school they are seeking to promote. The importance of the creation
of a marketing culture and the various techniques for establishing
effective internal communication which are discussed earlier in the
book, are especially relevant here (see chapter 4).

In the quest for stories, the school's publicity officer must be
unremittingly vigilant. Staff and pupils must be encouraged to
bring to the publicity officer's attention all potentially relevant
material which beneficially and positively promotes the school:
examination results, personal accomplishments, extra-curricular
activities, and so on, are all fodder for the media machine. And
the publicity officer must occasionally take the initiative to 'create'
potential media material. When Manor Park School heard that
Emlyn Hughes was visiting Nuneaton, they immediately invited
him to the school. He willingly accepted. And the media attention
generated by his visit gave the school a major corporate publicity
coup; it was able proudly to boast its sporting links – not to
mention show off the school's outstanding sports facilities.

It is worth noting another activity which will help a school gain media coverage for the purpose of PR: undertaking a survey and seeking to publish the results from it. Though not strictly a story, survey findings are of immense interest to editors. The school publicity officer might, therefore, consider encouraging pupils to undertake a small-scale, empirical investigation, using a field survey, into any acceptable issue or topic which is of interest to them; for example, attitudes of fellow pupils towards a number of specified social issues of the day, pupils' purchasing behaviour and views on material items of interest to the younger generation, and so on. Findings from surveys such as these will generate potential media material.

Managing media stories   Stories about pupils and the school, then, are potential sources of PR material. But in order to ensure that media coverage actually benefits the school, the process must be carefully managed. This involves maintaining an appropriate balance of publicity activities. To achieve this, the school's publicity officer should assiduously plan, coordinate and meticulously record all publicity activities. To provide a basis for appraising potential stories, a safe/dangerous publicity scale can be used (see figure 9.1). In this context a safe story: is one which is considered respectable; reflects substantial achievement; is manifestly serious in nature and explicitly connected with educational values and activities; and is non-controversial, i.e. unlikely to challenge the audiences' values. On balance, it is highly probable that the reader/viewer will be receptive towards the story.

Conversely, a dangerous story is essentially non-serious, unrelated or only implicitly connected with educational activities, and controversial. Here audience reaction is generally unpredictable, though sometimes antipathetic or hostile. For this reason, dangerous stories are potentially counter-productive and it is therefore imperative that they are very carefully managed indeed. Moreover, creating and managing such stories requires considerable skill (and sometimes nerve) on the part of the school's publicity officer. The dangerous story, however, is usually in considerable demand by editors and may secure wider media coverage. Ideally, a school should strive to publicize stories which, over a period of time, cover most of the positions on the scale in figure 9.1. Such a policy has been pursued successfully at Pindar Secondary School in Scarborough.

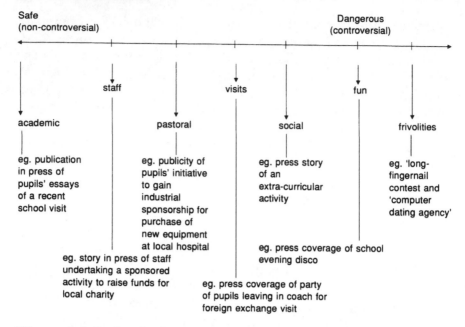

Figure 9.1 Scale of safe/dangerous media stories for schools
Source: Adapted from Mike Tilling, Press and Public Relations in Education',
Sheffield in Education Management, Sheffield City Polytechnic, Sheffield, 1988,
p. 11.

The safe/dangerous scale, then, provides a practical basis for selecting potential stories. It also offers a criterion for ascertaining which of them, i.e. those in the dangerous category, need especially close monitoring in order that evasive action might be taken, should it seem necessary. Clearly, the scale cannot provide a high degree of precision in this matter. It does offer, however, a general rule-of-thumb measure against which the possible risk associated with media coverage of school stories can be roughly gauged. Reference to some recent specific stories which can be located at each end of the safe/dangerous scale demonstrates the operational value of this technique.

An illustration of a relatively safe story is 'Visit filmed for TV' which was published in the *Scarborough Evening News* early Autumn 1987. This presented an interesting, non-controversial story of the activities of two pupils from Pindar School. It would be located at the 'academic' point on the scale.

Moving toward the other end of the safe/dangerous scale, Pindar School secured publication of a number of controversial articles, i.e. stories that are located in the fun and frivolities categories. An article entitled 'Nicola nails her mates in contest,' which described the result of a 'who's got the longest fingernails' competition, appeared in the *Scarborough Evening News* on 26 October 1987. It typifies the dangerous story, given its controversial theme. Fortunately for Pindar, the school derived only benefit from publication of the story: it acquired useful publicity without any apparent adverse reaction from readers. But on another occasion that term, Pindar School was less lucky.

In September, 1987, pupils at Pindar launched a computer dating project through the school's magazine, *Pindar Post*. The story was snapped up by the local press when the issue was first presented to them. Following the first 'match' in early October, 1987, the *Scarborough Evening News* enthusiastically took up the issue. A few days later, the *Scarborough Evening News* continued the romantic story with 'Pupils' first-class date, by which time, regional and national media were showing interest in the *Pindar Post*'s computer dating activities. Yorkshire Television covered the story, as did some other major regional media. So far, so good! Positive publicity for Pindar School. But the attendant danger in a story such as this, was about to break. Claiming the 'love-match' to be ill-founded, the *Daily Mirror*, (8 October, 1987) condemned the school newspaper's dating computing as matching not a pair of affectionate, romantic, fun-loving youngsters, but two people of whom one hated the other

Establishing repository for future stories   Another aspect of managing the school's publicity involves compiling a bank of stories for use when inspiration or source material for composing press releases and features articles temporarily dry up. In this way, the publicity officer can ensure the school sustains its public profile. Here, appropriate stories will be those which have a long-term as opposed to immediate interest. Relevant photographs should also be retained for future publicity (for guidance, see the section above 'Illustrative material').

Exhibiting pupils' work

Hitherto the discussion has centred on PR activities that have largely been derived from staff initiatives. Though pupils have played a part in this process, they have not been prime movers. But publicity can also be gained from a more direct involvement of pupils – by exhibiting their work in public places. There are a number of obvious outlets for this activity: visually impressive wall displays in main entrance/foyer to school; exhibits of pupils' artistic efforts in local shops; distribution of school magazine in the community; and presentation of pupils' work at schools' trade fair.

School foyer/reception entrance   Perhaps one of the most visually important aspects of a school to the visitor is the main reception entrance or foyer. The visitor's first impression of the school will be unduly influenced by the ambiance of its reception area or foyer which communicates powerful messages about it to outsiders.

The reception entrance/foyer should be attractive and welcoming, a fact evidently recognized by many hundreds of primary, junior and secondary schools who invest heavily in terms of time and energy in this physical feature of their institution. By using wall displays of pupils' artistic and creative work, photographs of school events, newspaper cuttings, and so on, a congenial atmosphere can be created. Attention to decor and comfortable furnishings will complete the effect. In this way, an invaluable additional input to the school's PR effort can be made.

Shop window displays   Local shops might be persuaded to provide window space for pupils' creative work, provided it is of high standard and well mounted. Local building societies and supermarkets are sometimes willing to help in this respect. In Scarborough, for example, several building societies recently displayed artistic work by a number of pupils at Pindar High School. And in Nuneaton the supermarket ASDA agreed to provide space to exhibit examples of creative work by pupils of Manor Park School.

School magazines   The value of school magazines as a vehicle for enhancing the effectiveness of a school's internal communications is discussed earlier in the book. But school magazines also help PR. Stories and articles about pupils' interests, hobbies and activities at school can be expressed through the magazine, and when circulated widely contribute to the effectiveness of a school's PR activities. Manor Park School's magazine *Community News*, for example, as its title suggests, is targeted at internal and external audiences: pupils, teachers, parents, governors, local politicians, shopkeepers, library readers, and many other sections of the community. With a circulation of over 2,000, the School's termly publication has proved an effective PR vehicle.

Schools' trade fair

Another useful PR tool is the trade fair, of which there are several permutations: 'industry fair', 'careers convention', 'young enterprise exhibition', 'schools' exhibition' are some of them. Essentially, it represents a desire on the part of the school to attain visibly close links with local community and industry/commerce.

A schools' trade fair provides participants who represent local industry, media, charities, local shops and small businesses, with opportunities to promote their organizations. For the sponsoring school, it brings members of the community in to meet pupils and staff in their working environment. Of key importance is the exhibiting of pupils' work, and in this context, high-quality wall and stand displays are vital. The school becomes the focus of attention: an almost unrivalled corporate publicity opportunity.

A schools' trade fair requires meticulous advance planning and organization; it is not unusual to need a preparation period of between 12 and 24 months. It is important to secure the moral and financial support of local industry and business early. Persuading a well-known personality or dignitary to attend will lend an air of credibility and legitimacy to the fair, thus increasing its public appeal. It is vital to ensure that the fair is given adequate publicity well in advance, including press coverage and mail shots to interested parties. It is important, too, that editors of all local and regional media receive invitations to attend, and are sent follow-up mail shots reminding them a few days prior to the event. On the day, it is important to ensure that maximum opportunity is taken to publicize the fair.

Telephone

By maintaining periodic telephone contact with parents, supplemented by written correspondence where necessary, some schools have successfully enhanced their corporate publicity efforts. Clearly, this activity must be undertaken with tact and sensitivity (so as not to alarm or offend parents), but can prove useful in conveying a concerned and caring attitude toward the pupil. Moreover, maintaining contact with parents in this way also promotes vital quality control and marketing research objectives, details of which are discussed elsewhere in the book.[7] Often, parents' initial enquiries about a school are by telephone. In this context, it forms one of the main channels of communication between potential 'buyers' and school. It therefore seems obvious that, in the interest of good PR, special attention should be given to this aspects of corporate communication. And Carolyn McGill stresses the importance of the telephone in PR when she advocates that we: 'Tape the word "opportunity" to each telephone. When the phone rings, the word will remind answerers to make a good first impression and to present themselves in a positive way'.[8]

Other activities

Consideration should be given also to open days/evenings. These facilitate liaison and verbal contact between school and parents. They also contribute to the realization of PR objectives.

Another relatively new but successful innovation in schools' PR activities, is the 'business lunch'. School dining facilities are used to entertain representatives of business, local politics and other key external groups. Birchwood Community School regularly hosts local industrialists and has gained considerable PR benefit from it (see the section 'Schools' trade fair' above). Obviously, catering and dining accommodation must be of a high standard. While some schools presently enjoy facilities of this order, many more have the potential to reach it. A recent coveted award to Pindar School in Scarborough, in recognition of the outstanding quality of its lunchtime fare, attests to this (the author confirms: his visit to Pindar during research for this book earned him a meal there).

Key points

1 PR involves informing parents, pupils and public about the school, not its products.
2 PR is valuable to a school's marketing effort because it

- raises the school's public profile
- is financially affordable

- publicizes the school's corporate identity
- can be used advantageously to change peoples' perception of the school
- is ethical
- offers reassurance to those associated with the school

3 The success of a school's PR programme is dependent on

- careful planning
- participation of all staff and pupils
- commitment of all staff and pupils to its objectives
- all staff and pupils being aware of it and appreciative of their respective role and expected contribution to its delivery
- compatibility with prevailing educational values and mores

4 There are a number of activities relevant to PR:

- press releases
- press receptions
- media stories and feature articles
- exhibitions of pupils' work
- schools' trade fair
- telephone

Notes

1 F. Jefkins, *Dictionary of Marketing Communication*, International Textbook Co. Ltd., UK, 1973, p. 86.
2 M. Tilling, *Press and Public Relations in Education*, Sheffield Papers in Education Management, Sheffield City Polytechnic, 1988, p. 10.
3 James Hodge, *Face The Press*, Management Update, 1986, p. 5.
4 According to Jefkins, 'In Britain usual to limited PR to educational, informative non-persuasive communication. Americans less inhibited about selling than British, and tend to associate PR more broadly with techniques of persuasion which more properly apply, in Britain, to advertising and propaganda'. F. Jefkins, *Dictionary*, p. 86.
5 Publicity items such as PR are, *vis-à-vis* advertising, considered more effective at reaching target audiences. On the whole, publicity is usually of greater interest to audiences because it (1) is perceived as 'news'; (2) also reaches those who do not notice

advertisments, and (3) is regarded generally as more credible. See, for example, W. M. Kincaid, *Promotion: Products, Services and Ideas*, Merrill, Ohio, USA, 1980, p. 329.

6 Ibid., p. 327.

7 See relevant sections in chapters 5 and 17.

8 Carolyn McGill, cited in Palmer Practice Management Report, 640 Wildwood Drive, Aurora, IL 60506, USA; quoted also in journal *Communication Briefings*, vol. 8, no. 2, 1989, Pitman, NY, USA.

10

Advertising

St George's Church of England School near Birmingham recently became the first school to advertise on TV – its six 20-second TV slots, which were preceded by press advertising and supplemented subsequently by group Church meetings (personal selling), resulted in 50 percent increase in admissions.[1]

Advertising is designed to inform parents (customers) and their children (consumers) about a specified school and to influence their 'buying' behaviour towards it. This activity forms part of a communication mix; as such it aims to reinforce the promotion efforts of the other constituents, i.e. corporate publicity or PR and personal selling (figure 10.1). These, in turn, underpin advertising activities: all are mutually supportive and interconnected. In this context, advertising performs both persuasive and promotional functions.

Role of Advertising

In the context of education and the communication mix, *product advertising* has a number of explicit roles. These are to:

- *inform* parents and pupils about educational opportunities (places and scholarships), products (special features of curriculum, teaching methods, etc.), and events (open days/evenings, exhibitions, PTA meetings, etc)
- *induce* parents to make further enquiries about a school with a view to seeking a place for their children
- *promote* awareness of a specified school and the benefits it offers pupils

● *underpin* other elements of the communication mix, for example, PR and personal selling

The principal purpose of corporate advertising, aspects of which are discussed in the preceding chapter, is to promote a school's image and corporate identity and 'put it on the map'; here, it complements the promotional activities described in chapters 8 and 9. Finally, schools also undertake staff advertising, which covers both teaching and support personnel.

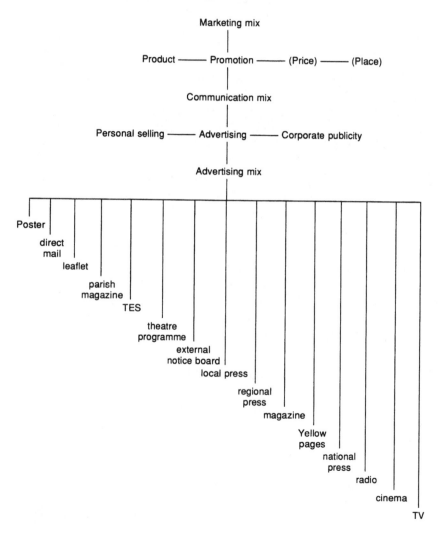

Figure 10.1 The advertising mix

Advertising Campaign: Planning and Implementation

Advertising works by matching message, advertising medium and target audience.[2] In order to successfully conjoin these three elements, the school must scrupulously plan, manage and coordinate its advertising campaign. Alternatively, the school may prefer to engage the services of an independent consultant, some of whom have acquired considerable experience and expertise in advertising for schools. By using their services for two terms, a school may amass sufficient knowledge to subsequently undertake its own advertising; a good consultant endeavours to put him/herself out of business by giving clients' sufficient confidence to eventually undertake necessary marketing tasks in-house. It is worth noting that most education marketing consultants actually save their clients considerable sums of money by ensuring that any advertising undertaken is appropriate for the intended target market.

Where a school opts for DIY advertising, however, the following sequential stages in planning and implementing an advertising campaign, may prove helpful:

- define target audience
- design message
- choose medium or combination of media
- decide timing and frequency of message
- place advertisment
- expedite all enquiries
- cost and measure effectiveness of advertisment

Defining the target audience

Successful advertising of school events, open days, places, entrance examinations, and staff vacancies, is dependent upon a clearly defined market audience, without which accurate targeting of the school's message is improbable. A school's existing knowledge of relevant market segments, supplemented where necessary with desk and field research, will usually suffice for this purpose. Conversely corporate advertising, where a specified school is the subject of, for example, a special magazine feature, demands less exacting market intelligence since specific messages are not targeted at single, discrete segments, but aimed at a broader audience.

Message

When undertaking construction of the advertising message, answers to three key questions should be sought:

What is (are) the derived benefit(s) from attending your school (i.e. what advantage(s) will a pupil gain from your school's product relative to those offered by competitors)?

What is it that your school's product does from which one or more benefits accrue?

What does the derived benefit mean to the client (i.e. is (are) the derived benefit(s) unequivocal to parents and pupils)?

The persuasiveness of a school advertisment is greatly enhanced where *benefits* and *quality* are made explicit. To illustrate this point, note two selling points which frequently feature in school advertisments:

'Small classes'

and

'Staff/pupil ratio 1:10'

Ostensibly, these descriptions seem satisfactory. But do they really convey benefits? A more apt description of these attributes might be:

'Personal attention'

In this way, it focuses the reader's mind quite specifically on a key, intangible quality which the education product offers. An advertisement for Walden Lincoln School offers a striking example of the way in which benefits might be powerfully conveyed. This advertisment appeared in the *New York Times* early in 1990.

The Walden Lincoln School building on 75 years of educational tradition

Walden Lincoln is for the family that demands . . .

- a carefully developed program that stresses academic achievement through cooperative exploration and discovery.
- a supportive and structured environment that encourages individual students to reach their full potential.
- a place where children learn to love learning.

The Walden Lincoln School
a coeducational day school for three year-olds through 12th grade

Another proven method of highlighting benefits is the use of testimonies of current pupils or alumni. A number of schools have recently adopted this practice to great effect.

In order to maximize the effectiveness of the school's advertising message, it is important also that it is perceptibly relevant and clear to the target audience. Failure to take account of this immutable rule caused consternation at Harris City Technology College (CTC) in Croydon, when its publicized mission of becoming a 'centre of excellence' became misconstrued as elitism: the college's principal admitted 'I was a bit surprised about people's misconceptions about us being an elite organization, creaming off a 180 students from the locality'. To which his colleague added: 'I felt there was confusion in people's minds. They couldn't equate the phrase "centre of excellence", which is something CTCs purport to be, with the statement we were making here at Harris that we're recruiting right across the ability range'.[3]

It is essential, too, that the advertisment message is succinct, simple, states unequivocally its purpose, and indicates how the reader should respond to it by giving contact name, address and telephone number. Moreover, consideration should be given to design and layout of the advertisement to ensure it stands out from those of its rivals and, in the case of newspapers and magazines, that its location in the publication is propitious. Finally, the content of the advertisment must conform to the advertising profession's code of conduct (see chapter 16).

Choosing the advertising medium

Advertising media form a critical link between message and audience. In order to facilitate this connection, consideration should be given to three key factors. First, in choosing an advertising medium, account must be taken of the characteristics of the target

High

Accuracy in reaching target audience

Leaflet *+
fund-raising appeals events, open
days/evenings; (distribution:
attach car windscreens,
households by hand, pupils to
take home)

Poster *+
open-days/evening,
events, exhibitions, fund-raising
appeals; (distribution: post office,
entrance to youth club, shop
windows)

Local Press *+
places, scholarships,
entrance, examinations,
staff vacancies

**External notice
board/canvas
information sheet** +
events, appeals, open
days/school perimeter adjoining
public highway/road)

Parish magazine *+
places, scholarships, entrance
examinations, events, appeals,
open days/evenings

Direct Mail *
events, appeals, open
days/evenings, promotional
material

Professional journal +
e.g. *TES* staff vacancies

Regional press *+
staff vacancies, places
scholarships, entrance
examinations (especially boarding
and top rank day schools)

National press *
staff vacancies, places,
scholarships and entrance
examinations for specialist
schools with national
catchment

Magazine *+
places, scholarships, entrance
examinations, promotional material

Theatre programme +
places, scholarships,
entrance examinations
open days/evenings

Yellow pages
general information and
name, address, telephone
number for enquiries and
prospectus

Radio
open
days/evenings,
fund-raising appeals,
exhibitions, events,
promotional material

Cinema
special appeals

Commercial TV
corporate
publicity, special
appeals

Low

Cost

High

Note
* suitable for conveying detailed information
+ specified advertising medium generally considered ethical by parents, teachers and governors.

Figure 10.2 Criteria for choosing advertising medium

audience ensuring that it is appropriate in terms of background, interests, values, attitudes and behaviour.

Second, thought should be given to the varying purposes of media, for each is concerned with achieving different objectives in the advertising process: some media are appropriate for corporate advertising (e.g. press release to help promote a school's identity), others are suitable for promoting product awareness (e.g. commercial radio to make known the government's Assisted Places Scheme), while a number of advertising media are more relevant for disseminating specific product information (e.g. poster advertising school open day).

Third, consideration should be given to detail and length of message in selecting medium. Owing to audiences' limited capacity to assimilate complex and voluminous data in short spaces of time, for example, TV and Cinema advertising is inappropriate for conveying detailed information, better for promoting general awareness of school and curriculum.

To help schools select the best medium or combination of media for advertising, figure 10.2 evaluates each in terms of relative cost and accuracy of targeting messages. Evidently, the most suitable media for advertising schools in terms of cost and accurate targeting are leaflets, posters and external notice boards. In this context, cinema and commercial TV are the least useful. While there are some novel advertising media not listed in figure 10.2 (Baverstock School in Kings Heath, Birmingham, for example, recently took advertising space on the exterior of West Midland Travel buses), most of the key methods are covered in the survey.

Deciding timing and frequency of message

Timing is key to successful school advertising. Messages should be targeted at relevant audiences when their decisions about schools are being made. In the case of secondary schools, selection is usually made between September and March. Where parental decisions about other types of schools are involved, or where circumstances are exceptional, then some variation in this time-scale may occur. That staff are available to deal with all enquiries generated from advertisments (from request for prospectus to asking for interview with head) must be taken into account when setting time-scale.

One possible time-scale and advertising mix for a (hypothetical) secondary school in the maintained sector wishing to advertise its sixth form (16+) provision is as follows:

Early October: LEA advertises Schools' Exhibition in local press and via leaflet distributed to all its secondary schools.

Late October: School participates in exhibition, having advertising literature and brochures available for distribution; School undertakes other related activities: builds database of visitors, undertakes personal selling, etc.

Early November: School advertises its 16+ provision, stressing benefits to pupils, in local newspaper. Prospectuses available for enquires. Mail shot (direct mail) to those on database compiled at late October exhibition above.

Mid-November: School repeats advertisment, but also announces dates for a pending open day/evening. Advertisment placed in local newspapers, local arts centre, theatre and museum programmes, libraries, youth clubs, sports centre and other relevant venues where relevant target market congregates. Prospectuses available for distribution and senior staff ready to deal with telephone enquiries. Key Target group: Schools without 16+ provision.

Penultimate week in November: School repeats above in local newspapers prior to open day/evening: a gentle reminder. Mail shot repeated.

Last week in November: School open day/evening. Number of key activities take place on the day: names and addresses of visitors noted to enhance/ update existing database; staff available to undertake personal selling; prospectuses and leaflets available for distribution; head teacher's address to visitors presents/reinforces positive image of the school, expounds the school's philosophy and emphasizes the benefits that pupils derive from it; number of representative senior pupils act as guides to visitors, thus revealing the 'end-product' of the school's education service; displays of pupils' work, etc; apt signage to create desired image and highlight school's selling points.

January: mail shot to those on database, inviting them to contact the school for further details, interview or application form.

Here it is evident that effective advertising cannot operate in isolation from other constituents of the communication mix: all are mutually supportive and interdependent. This illustration also indicates frequency of advertising exposure. Research has shown that, in the case of newspapers, radio and TV, three to five separate exposures are necessary before an advertising message will register with audiences. Generally, school advertising involves several different complementary media used at different times, according to when audiences are making decisions about education, or might be induced to contribute to or participate in school events.

Implementing an Advertising Campaign

If a school's advertising is to eventually generate firm enrolments, it is vital to facilitate action in the advertising/selling process. This involves simply responding positively and quickly to prospects' enquiries, either for prospectuses, other specific information, or interview. It is important that staff are on hand to deal with all enquiries generated by advertising. If the activity of responding to a specified advertisment can be made convenient or user-friendly, this may encourage parents to make further enquiries. Though likely to be considered too pushy by European standards in education (some institutions of higher education here use it), the pre-paid business reply card is employed not infrequently by north American schools.

Costing an advertising campaign

In contrast to PR, advertising makes considerable demands on a school's marketing budget (figure 10.2 above offers some guidance here). When planning a campaign, a number of factors should be taken into account: staff time spent discussing advertising campaign and undertaking preparation and detailed design work; if relevant, time preparing and discussing brief with advertising agency or consultant; cost of commissioning agency's/consultant's services; cost of buying space/viewing time/listening time in relevant media; cost of responding to enquiries generated from advertisments, postage, stamps, prospectuses, etc.; and cost of undertaking necessary research work.

Measuring effectiveness

Given that advertising is probably the most expensive promotion medium a school is likely to use, measuring the relative effectiveness of individual advertisments is important. While it is usually difficult to evaluate the impact of this activity with any real precision, a number of techniques are available to measure the persuasive and promotional effects of school advertising.

The impact of education advertisments on target audiences can be undertaken using aided and unaided recall. Here, respondents are asked in survey interviews to indicate how much they can recall about a recent specified advertisment. Respondents are either prompted (aided) or not (unaided) by the interviewer:

Another approach to measuring the impact of advertising is by using before and after surveys. Here, questionnaires are used to assess the degree to which clients' perception of a school or its product has changed following an advertising campaign. This is especially valuable, for example, in gauging the effectiveness of corporate advertising.

A further method of evaluating the effectiveness of advertising involves comparing the respective number of enquiries from two different advertisments for the same school. This approach has been used with considerable effect by a large number of schools in the USA and some colleges and universities here.[4]

In certain circumstances, it is judicious to pre-test a planned education advertisment on a typical target audience, thus minimizing the risk of failure. Inviting staff and pupils to participate in this process is worth considering. Keeping records of where earlier advertisments had been placed and the number of responses to each will help the school construct a profile of the best media for its future advertising.

Key points

1 Advertising educators' products aims to:

- convert
- reinforce

2 Product advertising performs a number of important functions:

- informing prospects
- inducing prospects to make further enquiries about a school's products
- helping schools gain access to new market segments and retain existing ones
- promoting awareness of benefits education products offer
- helps underpin other elements in the communication mix

3 Corporate advertising performs a key function:

to promote a school's image and corporate identity, i.e. put it
on the map

4 In planning and designing its advertising, a school must undertake a number of discrete, interconnected activities:

- define target audience
- construct content and design of advertisment
- select appropriate medium or combination of media
- decide timing and frequency of message(s)
- measure the effectiveness of advertisments

5 The effectiveness of education advertisments can be measured
by:

- aided and unaided recall surveys
- before and after analysis
- counting and comparing the number of enquiries generated by
individual or specified advertisments

Notes

1 The advertisement for St George's Church of England School
in Birmingham first appeared on Central Television on Sunday,
13 February 1990, at 8.30 p.m.
2 F. Jefkins, *Dictionary of Marketing Communication*, International
Textbook Co. Ltd., UK., 1973, p. 2
3 BBC 1, *Clean Slate*, week beginning 12 February 1990.
4 The Open University used this method to appraise the impact
on prospects of two advertisements. It used two advertisements,
distinguished only by a different visual illustration, on two separate occasions in the same newspaper, the *Daily Mirror*. In one
advertisement, a visual illustration of a cap and gown was used,
but not in the other; in all other respects the advertisments were
identical. The cap and gown approach generated a 15 per cent
higher response rate than the other, a difference of nearly 5,000
extra enquiries. Other promotion tools also contributed to this
outcome, for example, the university's PR campaign, but it
serves to demonstrate how the relative impact of advertising can
be measured.

11

Fund-raising

[There] will undoubtedly be pressure on heads to raise funds by direct appeal to parents or to local industry . . . if we are not careful we shall find the creation of a new breed of head . . . the charismatic charmer who can get sponsorship out of local industry.[1]

Introduction

By utilizing communication skills and enthusiasm of teachers, pupils, governors and parents, many schools are able to resource their marketing activities. Sometimes, however, it becomes necessary to seek additional funds for this purpose. An obvious source of revenue is a school's education budget, but this is likely to prove contentious, as the National Association of Head Teachers (NAHT) suggest: 'any marketing expenditure (must be set) at levels which are designed not to disadvantage present pupils'.[2] Evidently, how far each school dips into its education budget for marketing purposes is, as the NAHT advises, a matter for the respective head to 'consider whether this is the best use of finances which could otherwise have been devoted to providing additional resources for the school'.[3] In view of this expressed concern a search for another source of revenue seems both politic and practical. This chapter briefly considers three proven methods of income generation for schools: fund-raising, seeking sponsorship and utilizing capital assets.

Fund-raising

In contrast to North American schools, where there exists an established fund-raising culture, British educational institutions are generally circumspect towards this form of income generation. But fund-raising is slowly gaining legitimacy here and many schools now recognize its value in enhancing their future resource needs.

Recently, Oxford University demonstrated convincingly how fruitful a long-term fund-raising campaign can be. Its skilfully managed 'Campaign for Oxford' succeeded in raising millions of pounds to help resource existing and future education and research programmes. Though the scale of Oxford's formidable fund-raising initiative contrasts sharply with the distinctly modest campaigns individual schools are likely to pursue, the principles from which the university's success is derived are generic to all income-generation activities. Prerequisites for successful fund-raising are planning, generating ideas and publicity.

Planning

Here, consideration should be given to organization, research, formulating goals and objectives, and planning strategy.

Organization This aspect of planning involves the establishment of two features in a school's organization: a fund-raising/development officer, and effective internal communications.

Overall responsibility for initiating, implementing, coordinating and monitoring fund-raising activities should be undertaken by an experienced staff member. By so doing, it will be possible to closely manage all processes and stages involved here: from inculcating a positive attitude on the part of staff towards fund-raising, to enlisting the willing and active support of colleagues and pupils early in any fund-raising campaign.

In order to engage and sustain the interest and commitment of staff and pupils in fund-raising, an appropriate system of communication must be in place. The relevant institutional arrangement for promoting effective internal communication, which is discussed in detail in chapter 4, comprise:

attitudinal change	commitment from the top, and enhancement of staff morale
structural change	simplification of line management, accessible senior management, communal staff facilities, noticeboards, school magazines, newsletters and daily news sheets

activities for change   expression of messages in appropriate form,
                         staff meetings, team briefings and consultation

Desk research   It is vital that the school's development officer has
all information to undertake detailed planning for fund-raising.
Desk research will facilitate this end: it will generate data to

- select the most propitious time for launch of campaign
- identify target audience(s) most likely to contribute to fund and select
  strategy for reaching them
- identify those 'causes' people are most willing to support
- gauge target audiences' likely financial contribution to the campaign
- ascertain whether (and how many) other schools and non-profit organizations are currently involved in fund-raising – the sum total of
  peoples' disposable income available for fund-raising is finite

Evidently fund-raising is a highly competitive business. There is,
however, a yearly variation in donations made to non-profit organizations, a typical pattern of which is shown in figure 11.1.
Here it can be seen that income from donations, while generally consistent, fluctuates according to, for example, settlement
of company accounts when contributions to charities are made
(April and September), or when local authorities distribute
funds (February). By taking account of peaks and troughs in
charity donations, a school is able to plan its fund-raising more
judiciously.

It is essential to identify relevant mechanisms by which parents
and benefactors might contribute to the school's fund-raising endeavours and make known these various facilities to them. A
number of convenient methods to facilitate contribution to schools'
fund-raising needs are available at present:

Deed of Covenant   Where the school is a registered charity, and
the contributor a UK tax payer, the school will be able to claim
back from the Inland Revenue tax paid on the money covenanted;
at present, the school may reclaim £33 for every £100 covenanted.
Covenants are payable under instalment or single payment schemes
and can be made by individuals or companies. Contributions,
however, must be for a period of time which exceeds 3 years (i.e.
a minimum of 3 years, 1 day); most schools encourage parents to
set up a deed of covenant for 4 years. Details of Deed of Covenant
are available from the Inland Revenue.

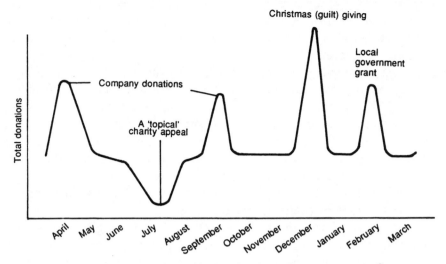

Figure 11.1 Typical yearly variation in donation to non-profit organizations
Source: Gillian Hollins and Bill Hollins, *Total Design: Managing the Design Process in the Service Sector*, Pitman, London, 1991, p. 99.

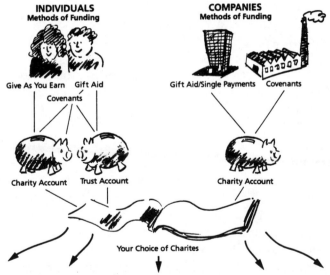

Figure 11.2 How a CAF account works
Source: Charities Aid Foundation, Tonbridge, Kent. Used with permission.

Give-As-You-Earn Scheme which permits parents to contribute £50 per month or some combination equal to £600 per annum. Here, the sum of money is paid to the school by the parent's employer or agency acting on its behalf. Under the scheme, no further tax refund is available to the school, but the contribution can be varied at will, thus providing, vis-a-vis other schemes, more flexibility to parents.

Life-time Gifts over £400 lump sum qualify for Gift Aid The school is deemed to have received £533 pro rata and can therefore re-claim £133 in tax. Under this contribution scheme, payments are usually exempt from Capital Gains and Inheritance Tax. Any gift to a charity, made during life-time or on death, is generally exempt from inheritance tax. In North America, many educational institutions derive pecuniary gifts from alumni. Here, some schools target their message for support at parents with children who are in the early stages of their education career.

Miscellaneous The Finance Act, 1991, permits a gift by a trader to an educational establishment for its trading activities to attract no further tax charge in the hands of either the trader or the school. (Note: In each case, then, where the tax payer is permitted to deduct the gift from income, tax will be saved at the tax payer's highest rate.)

CAF Parents might prefer to contribute by using the facilities offered by Charities Aid Foundation (CAF) (CAF, 48 Pembury Road, Tonbridge, Kent, TN9 2JD, Tel: 0732 771333). In effect, CAF acts as a bank to assist its account holders to make contributions to charities of their choice. Both individuals and companies are eligible to open a CAF account. Figure 11.2 illustrates how the system works.

Formulating campaign objectives It is vital that clear and worthy/legitimate objectives are set for fund-raising activities and that these are communicated to staff, pupils, parents and those public whose support the school seeks. Moreover, it is equally important that progress in any fund-raising event is fed back to all concerned, especially parents and other contributors. The outcome or development of fund-raising events for the purpose of constructing tangible projects, such as building a new school sports pavilion or similar, is easily communicated to its supporters.

A statement of campaign objectives serves a number of practical ends:

● it provides a measure against which campaign performance can be assessed, thus, if applicable, warning of need to adjust strategy

- it indicates required level of resources in terms of staff time, materials, renting accommodation, and related matters
- it offers a basis for allocating and clearly communicating to staff and pupils participating in the fund-raising event, their respective tasks and responsibilities

The purpose of any fund-raising event must be meritorious and its objectives realistic. Staff, pupils, parents and public should feel a campaign is worth their time and money; Henley-in-Arden High School's parachute jump, which aimed to generate funds for purchase of new technical equipment (and which is described in chapter 9), epitomizes the legitimate fund-raising cause. And given the obvious resource implications of fund-raising, objectives must be achievable; a maximum of one or two campaigns per year is manageable for most schools.

Strategy Here consideration is given to the *means* by which fund-raising objectives are realized. In this context, relevant target audiences must be identified and appropriate communications designed to reach them; much of the material presented in chapter 10 is relevant here.

An effective fund-raising strategy was undertaken by an established independent preparatory school, which initiated an appeal to raise funds for major building works. An attractive handbook was produced by the school to explain to potential contributors the objectives of the appeal and to provide relevant organizational details. A run-down of its contents illustrates the sort of information which encourages potential contributors:

Introduction by the chairman of the governors
The whole project: phase by phase summary
Architects' plan
Aerial perspective: architects' model
Letter from the headmaster
List of appeal committee
Methods of donating
Statement of target
Deed of covenant form

Generating fund-raising ideas

It is important to encourage colleagues and pupils to participate in the creation of ideas for new and novel fund-raising events.

Both groups of participants are key sources of inspiration. Ideas can be gleaned also from observing other schools' fund-raising endeavours.

There are many proven, reliable fund-raising activities which accompany school fêtes, fairs and open days: plastic duck racing, lotteries, tombola, prizes, etc.[4]

In order to maximize support, schools may seek novel fund-raising themes. There are plenty of good ideas around. One unusual fund-raising activity is described as a 'truffle trot' which is held every year in Eugene, Oregon, USA, around Valentine's Day. This event, which raises funds for a specified charity, requires participants paying a $10 registration in return for a chocolate truffle and an obligatory T-shirt. Simply, the 'more calories burned, the more you can earn. Chocolate prizes are awarded'.[5] The International Carole Kai Bed Race in Honolulu is another extraordinary fund-raising idea. Taking place over two days and generating almost $100,000 yearly, it involves racing contestants through the streets on beds.[6] And some schools in this country have recently demonstrated their capacity to launch innovative fund-raising activities.[7] Whatever ideas are selected for a school fund-raising event, it is important they manifest a number of characteristics. Essentially, fund-raising activities must be

- interesting to staff, pupils, parents and the local community
- as far as practical, unusual or novel
- inherently attractive to staff, pupils, parents and the local community

Notwithstanding the proven value of some of the fund-raising events listed above to generating income, the most effective means of achieving this objective is a proficiently organized appeal.

Publicizing fund-raising events and appeals

If fund-raising is to achieve its objectives, the event or appeal must be well publicized: it is vital that everyone knows about it and is told why it is taking place. Again, reference to Henley-in-Arden High School's press release, which is discussed in chapter 9, attests to the importance of informing all potentially interested parties about a fund-raising event/appeal and the reasons for it.

Fund-raising campaigns must be marketed both internally and externally. The campaign message should be targeted at all staff and pupils, and key audiences such as parents and local community. Their support is essential to the success of the fund-raising event or appeal.

Sponsorship

Modern sponsorship is 'a mutually beneficial business arrangement between sponsor and sponsored to achieve a defined objective'.[8] It involves also 'the provision of financial or material support (a) for some independent activity which is not intrinsic to the furtherance of commercial aims, but (b) from which the supporting company might reasonably hope to gain commercial benefit'.[9] Sponsorship is not a form of corporate or product advertising, does not consist of patronage, nor form part of the sponsor's main commercial function.

Motivation for sponsorship

For schools, this 'mutually beneficial relationship' is manifest in terms of, for example, 'brochures, the supply of sports vests for school teams bearing the name of the school and some mention of the identity of the sponsor to the offer of agencies such as insurance or financial services with a percentage return to the school'.[10] Specific illustrations of recent successful sponsorship in schools, and the benefits that accrued to them, include the following:[11]

School	Sponsoring company	Benefit
Birchwood High Small Health, Birmingham	British Nuclear Fuels	Prospectus
	Barclays Bank	Colour brochure
	Casio	Re-equipped music room
	Save & Prosper	New roof, interior decoration
Manor Park Comprehensive, Nuneaton	Triton	Promotional materials
Leading secondary, Milton Keynes	Barclays Bank	£1 for every pupil opening account with Barclays

Longsands Community College, St Neots, Cambridgeshire	Alliance & Leicester Building Society	Free Filofax for each pupil
Numerous schools	Shell UK	Fact sheets on energy and oil
Numerous schools	Texas Instruments	Information pack relating to company's field of interest
Numerous schools	Tesco; ICI; Pentax	Educational/information packs and materials

For the sponsor, assisting schools in this way offers a number of marketing opportunities:

- it helps gain recognition as good corporate citizen
- it opens up channels of communication with young people – tomorrow's key consumers and employees
- it enhances corporate image and promotes product awareness

In order to promote further understanding of corporate motivation in matters of sponsorship, figure 11.3 provides a basis on which a typical company might roughly assess the potential value of materially supporting schools. Using a score out of 10 points, the company places a value on each sponsorship project/proposal according to the probability that it satisfies a number of specified corporate needs. Though designed to assist the sponsor, this construction offers schools more insight to the likely considerations made by companies when choosing between competing requests for sponsorship.

In effect, when a company assesses the value to it of offering sponsorship to a school, it looks for synergy between the event or purpose for which the school seeks sponsorship and its own corporate values. It seems that the more people can be told about how the sponsor's activity is used to support an event the more the sponsor is likely to derive the benefit of increased goodwill towards it.[12] Evidently, the extent to which a school can demonstrate its willingness and ability to make explicit the connection between the sponsored event and the company, the more successful its request for support is likely to be.

Characteristic of potential sponsorship	A Score out of 10 pts	B Weighting	C Total
Natural link with sponsor's product or service		× 3	30
Aptness to corporate image		× 2	20
Identification of audience with sponsor's selected targets		× 3	30
Chairman's personal interest		× 1	10
Geographical links with sponsor's business		× 2	20
Benefit to sponsor's current community relations activities		× 1	10
Benefit to sponsor's staff relations		× 3	30
Aptness to sponsor's previous record in sponsorship		× 2	20
Potential advertising exposure		× 1	10
Potential press coverage		× 3	30
Potential television coverage		× 4	40

Total score (out of 250)

Instruction: Give each sponsorship characteristic a points valuation (out of 10) in the light of your own company's requirements. This score goes in column A. Multiply this score by the weighting figure in column B to obtain the possible score for each, and enter it in column C, which gives the possible maximum. At the foot of column C add up the total score out of 250.

Figure 11.3 Mechanism for assessing value of a potential sponsorship project.
Source: V. Head, Sponsorship, 1981, p. 90.

Approaching a sponsor

Companies who seek association with educational institutions usually initiate sponsorship relations with schools. But this is not always the case. Sometimes schools must induce external bodies to support them. If appeals for sponsorship are to succeed, however, a thorough grasp of the potential sponsor's corporate personality must be acquired. It is essential also that the initial approach to the organization is undertaken adroitly.

In selecting a potential sponsor, it is important that the school recognizes that it must offer the company concerned, in return for its support, a partnership which is 'attractive and relevant to (its) business style, marketing philosophy, corporate profile and so on'.[13] The school should endeavour to get to know the external organization and to understand its corporate mission, i.e. the sort of interests the company might hope to further by supporting it. In this way, it is possible to identify those companies that are willing to sponsor educational establishments: 'A knowledge of corporate strategies', writes Victor Head, 'gives vital clues to relevant sponsorships'.[14] Here, desk research is essential: Peter Walshe argues: 'Evidence in the form of good market research can dispel many of the myths and be extremely powerful in attracting new sponsors by "talking" to them in their own language'.[15]

Success in acquiring sponsorship is dependent also on the appropriateness of initial contact between school and company. Research will help identify the most effective method(s) of communication. Indeed this aspect cannot be overstated: it is imperative that both the company and those who represent it are thoroughly researched. Additionally, adherence to the following rather obvious rules will assist here:[16]

Initial approach should be by personal letter to the manager whose remit in the company covers sponsorship (ensure correspondence is correctly addressed).

Use school headed note paper for all correspondence with the company. Keep your letter reasonably brief.

Attempt to convey to the company a sense of honest and enthusiastic professionalism.

If the company responds encouragingly to your request, attempt to gain a face-to-face meeting with the company's representative; if at all possible, it is better to send two school staff to meet the company's representative.

Ensure that your correspondence communicates an understanding of the company's corporate interests, that the sponsorship project is viable, and contains all relevant information to aid the company's decision.

Utilizing Capital Assets

By utilizing capital and physical assets, a school can further supplement its revenue. School premises can be hired out when not in use during weekends and holidays; quality school lunches (of the prize-winning kind offered at Pindar School in Scarborough) might be offered to the community's senior citizens; local community activities, such as amateur dramatics, might welcome use of the school stage and facilities for their productions in return for a small fee; and corridors and reception/foyer areas can be used to sell advertising space to local shops and businesses. The experiences of Ann Arbor High School in Michigan, USA, attests to the potential income-generating potential of some school's capital assets. During Michigan University's home football matches, Ann Arbor High converts its playing fields into fee-paying car parks, which earns them in excess of $20,000 a week. And nearer to home, Peter Downes, who talks of a 'gentle entrepreneuralism' blossoming in Cambridgeshire schools, describes some interesting developments there:

> we happen to have a stately home which is part of the school, so obviously we are able to use that for wedding receptions and conferences, and banquets and seminars and so on, and for antique fairs which are particularly good.

Downes continues:

> But some of my colleagues who have less favoured environs than my own have found ways in which they can earn money as well. For example, one of my colleagues in the community college in Cambridgeshire has discovered that his college is actually on a long distance bus route. During the weekend he makes his playground available as a service station area and his parents come in and use the school kitchen facilities to serve meals and the school toilets are open, so he has a regular supply of long distance coaches which stop at his school and make use of the facilities.[17]

Evidently, the potential offered by school premises and facilities for income generation is almost interminable.

Key points

1 There are three proven methods for generating additional resources for marketing:

- fund-raising
- sponsorship
- utilizing school facilities and premises for income generation

2 Successful fund-raising is dependent on

- effective management and organization of event
- setting clear goals and objectives
- formulating appropriate strategies

- generation of ideas for new and novel events
- ensuring event is well publicized

3 Sponsorship is a mutually beneficial business arrangement be tween sponsor and school.
4 The mutual benefits from sponsorship are considerable.
5 The success of a school's sponsorship appeal to an external organization is dependent on, among other things a demonstrable synergy between the use to which funding will be put, including the ethos of the school, and the sponsor's corporate values and philosophy.
6 School facilities and premises, if imaginatively exploited, offer opportunities for additional income generation.

Notes

1 Peter Downes, *Managing Education in the 1990s – Local Management in Practice*, The Chartered Institute of Public Finance and Accountancy, October 1989, p. 13.
2 National Association of Head Teachers, *The Marketing of Schools* (Council Memorandum), National Association of Head Teachers, September 1990, para 3.5.
3 Ibid.
4 See especially G. Gorman, *Fund-Raising for Schools*, Kogan Page, London, 1988.
5 *Sunset Magazine*, Lane Publishing Co., 80 Willow Road, Menlow Park, CA 94025, USA.
6 Ibid.
7 Henley-in-Arden High School's parachute jump which is described in detail in chapter 9, is one obvious example here.
8 Victor Head, *Sponsorship: The Newest Marketing Skill*, Woodhead-Faulkner, in association with the Institute of Marketing, London, 1981, pp. 2–3.
9 Ibid. It is described further by Head as 'the donation or loan of resources . . . by private individuals or organisations to other individuals or organisations engaged in the provision of those public goods and services designed to improve the quality of life'. See Head, *Sponsorship*, p. 3.

10 Solihull Metropolitan Borough Council, Education Sub-Committee, Minutes of Meeting, Item 5, 'Sponsorship of Schools', 22 May, 1990.

11 Author's interviews; Marketing Week, vol. 13, no. 29, 28 September 1990.

12 Colin McDonald, 'Evaluating Sponsorship', *Survey*, vol. 7, no. 2, Summer 1990. There is, Colin McDonald stresses, 'much evidence of the importance of *product relevance* . . . Sponsorship must be *appropriate* and meet people's expectations, in several ways. It is in this "appropriateness", or goodness-of-fit, that sponsorship succeeds and must be measured', p. 8.

13 Victor Head, *Sponsorship*, p. 92.

14 Ibid., p. 96.

15 Peter Walshe, 'The Link', *Survey*, vol. 7, no. 2, Summer, 1990, p. 3.

16 For more detailed exposition, see Head, *Sponsorship*, p. 94.

17 P. Downes, *Managing Education*, pp. 8–9.

12

Education Exhibitions

These are essentially places where competing schools meet parents and prospective pupils for the purpose of disseminating detailed information about educational programmes and curricula. Exhibitions also provide vital opportunities for schools to undertake further PR, advertising, personal selling and marketing research.[1]

This form of marketing communication is rapidly gaining recognition and importance in education. The success of City of Birmingham's annual careers convention 'Beyond Sixteen' attests to their increased popularity. Thousands of prospective pupils and their parents in the locality have been able to undertake close scrutiny of a wide range of courses offered by participating schools and talk to representative teaching staff there. In the independent sector, schools' exhibitions organized by ISIS have also been well received over a number of years.

Value of Schools' Exhibitions

The value of exhibitions to schools is incontestable:

- they encourage and facilitate numerous potential pupils and their parents to meet staff/representatives of participating schools face-to-face,
- they provide a platform from which schools can present their respective institution and curriculum in an appealing and interesting light (i.e. they can facilitate corporate and product advertising)
- their visitors are, in effect, a captive and on the whole, responsive audience

- they enable participating schools to distribute immediately, on request, prospectuses and other relevant information to potential pupils and parents to help them choose
- they enable participating schools to present a more human, caring and responsive image, and make their curricula seem less abstract
- they enable schools to undertake valuable and inexpensive market research: schools are afforded instant and direct access to consumers, i.e. prospective pupils and parents who visit the stand.[2]

It is evident, then, that exhibitions assist schools to realize their promotional objectives. But visitors gain from exhibitions too, since they

- permit detailed and searching questions to be asked of participating schools
- provide a forum for prospective pupils and their parents to ask questions, seek elucidation or reassurance on matters relating to participating schools' education programmes and curricula
- offer them almost unrivalled opportunity to readily compare schools and their respective offerings

Managing and Presenting the School's Exhibition Stand

Generally, education exhibitions attract three categories of visitor: those with expressed preference for a particular school, but who seek confirmation or reassurance; parents/prospective pupils who consciously desist from choosing until all options have been examined, but possess a view of the defining characteristics of a good school; visitors with neither preconceived preferences for any participating school nor view of the defining characteristics of a good school.

Strictly, speaking each of the three categories of visitor demands slightly different strategies of an exhibitor to attract them to the stand. But realistically, it is better for participating schools to concentrate on the last two categories of visitor, and accordingly, adopt those strategies relevant to those segments. There are, however, two immutable rules which apply equally to all categories of visitor:

- the exhibition stand must be professionally managed, and seen to be so
- presentation of stand must be professional and of high quality

The importance of these two precepts derive from the highly competitive nature of education exhibitions as each school's stand vie for visitors' attention, and the observation that the exhibition visitor spends on average only 9 seconds at each stand – parents/prospective pupils must be attracted to the stand and their interest must be sustained.

Effective management of exhibition stand

This requires:[3]

- clear statement of objectives
- advance planning
- effective coordination of the various activities and inputs associated with running an exhibition stand
- staff who are presentable, enthusiastic, responsive and well informed (training should be given where necessary)
- voluminous supplies of brochures and literature for distribution, all clearly specifying name, address and telephone number of head teacher should parents require additional information, wish to visit the school or seek interview
- mechanism, for building database of names and addresses of enquirers for the purpose of sending follow-up materials/information about dates and times of open days/evenings
- performance appraisal to ascertain whether objectives have been achieved
- modification of stand to ameliorate perceptible weaknesses

Presentation

Most visitors to an education exhibition have put aside time to attend and are there specifically to seek out educational opportunities. But each school's stand is vying for the visitor's attention *vis-à-vis* those of other participants. Clearly, attention to a number of factors will help here:

- location of stand
- physical layout of stand and furniture, with special reference to seating arrangements and facilities for staff and visitors to talk
- quality and balance of display material with emphasis on professionalism of design and finish, all consistently displaying school logo or other corporate identity

- lighting, to highlight stand and key display materials, such as school logo, visual materials portraying aspects of school life, courses, examination results, etc.
- design and colour of backdrop, highlighting school logo, relevant visual displays
- layout of furniture
- friendly, enthusiastic, helpful and well-informed staff – key factor: this will be perceived by parents/prospective pupils as indicator/evidence of quality of teaching staff
- friendly, enthusiastic and helpful pupils/peer group representatives – key factor: this will be perceived by parents/prospective pupils as indicator of the end-product, i.e. how its pupils turn out, and how receptive its pupils are to new arrivals
- easily assimilated material readily accessible to visitor
- content of display material which gives visitor a feel for the place

Conclusion

Clearly, if a school were to incorporate all the above features in their exhibition stand, the likelihood of it achieving its set objectives are considerable. Some exhibition practitioners, such as Peter Cotterell, however, intimate that further activities might be necessary to ensure success. Addressing an audience of sixth form and further education college teachers, Cotterell suggested that the educationalist might consider introducing imaginative visual aids or gimmicks to differentiate their stand from those of competitors. Few schools, it seems, are likely to adopt Cotterell's extraordinary techniques – for school marketing they conjure a sense of impropriety – but the reader might find some of his imaginative methods interesting, such as the 'invisible prize cards' which is described here:

> You distribute the cards to all . . . [prospective pupils and parents] you want to see. The cards are printed with a message explaining that they offer the chance to win various prizes and that the prize the prospect has won is printed in an apparently empty box.
>
> The catch is that the name of the prize is printed in invisible ink. The only way the prospect can tell what he's [/she's] won is by having the box rubbed over with a special developing pen. And – you've guessed it – the only place to find such a pen is at your . . . exhibition stand.[4]

Key points

1 Exhibitions bring schools, prospective pupils and parents together for the purpose of respectively disseminating and gathering information about educational programmes on offer.
2 Educational exhibitions are growing in recognition and importance.
3 The value of exhibitions to schools is incontestable for a number of reasons.
4 Exhibitions bring benefits to their visitors, too.
5 The success of a school's exhibition stand, as measured against set objectives, is largely dependent on

- effective management
- quality of presentation

Notes

1 W. M. Kincaid, *Promotion: Products, Services and Ideas*, Merrill, Ohio, USA, 1980, see pp. 301–2
2 See B. G. Yovovich, 'Trade Show! Think of it as a magazine', *Advertising Age*, 23 April, 1979; see also S. Cavanaugh, 'Setting Objectives and Evaluating the Effectiveness of Trade Show Exhibits', *Journal of Marketing*, vol. 40, no. 4, October, 1976; and P. Cotterell, *The Exhibition Gold Mine*, Unibrand Training, London (pamphlet), undated.
3 See B. G. Yovovich, 'Trade Show', and S. Cavanaugh, 'Setting Ojectives'.
4 P. Cotterell, *The Exhibition Gold Mine*.

13

Case Study 1: Marketing Plan for a Secondary School

Introduction

During the 1980s, a group of student researchers were commissioned by the head of a large, maintained sector secondary school in England to undertake a detailed market analysis and prepare a marketing plan. Using appropriate research techniques, a study of the market was undertaken, the results formally written up and presented to the head. Appended to the submission document was a résumé or executive summary; this is reproduced here, without editorial modification.

This case study relates to the material covered in chapter 3 where methods and approaches to constructing a marketing plan is discussed. It illustrates the scope and scale of such a plan and lists key content: objectives; findings from SWOT analysis; gaps in market intelligence following SWOT analysis; ascertaining parents'/potential pupils' perception of the school; results from competitive analysis; identification of relevant market segments; specific strategic objectives; and methods for targeting specified market segments, and so on. Moreover, it reveals the type of solutions that might be appropriate for dealing with the school's problems – identified in the market research – i.e., the use of *promotion* to ameliorate the school's poor image.

The unexpurgated extract which is given here shows what is realistically achievable for most schools intending to write their own marketing plans.

Consultancy report: résumé

Setting objectives

Goals (short term) should be:

1 To attract more local children and parents.
2 Shift image from that of 'better at handling less able'.

Objectives (long term):

1 Discover and secure school's position within the total market.
2 Attract more custom so that we can select and recruit our desired students.
3 Become the market leader in the locality providing a fully comprehensive and coordinated education for present and potential customers.

SWOT analysis

This identifies and includes:

Strengths	e.g. low staff turnover
Weaknesses	e.g. low level of funding and maintenance; no formalized disciplinary procedures; academic results not particularly favourable; attracts less able children
Opportunities	e.g. external funding and rising population
Threats	e.g. local education authority restrictions

Information required

More research into parents' views
Customer analysis
Appraise position of competitors, e.g., SWOT analysis, press cuttings, prospectuses, reports, questionnaires.

Image

Among present and potential customers not altogether favourable; informal, solid foundation for less able, less impressive academic subject results – a circular effect.

Needs a shift to a more formal dynamic and team spirited image. New prospectuses promotes the facts and the caring image, it must reach its target audience of C1/C2s. Must maintain high profile locally through many and varied events/activities, e.g., exhibitions, competition.

Strategy

Become [pro-active] and exploit competitors' weaknesses. Refuse to accepts status quo, strive to be different.

Product

Survey of parents of 8–11 year olds want academic results, good teachers, discipline, good facilities, but not single sex. Grammar schools are favoured hence a grammar school education in a coeducational comprehensive environment.

Market segment (1)

63% of parents send a younger child to the same school as that attended by older sibling, hence this must be the key segment to target.

Ethical and financial limits inhibit targeting other main groups (older child at another secondary school, oldest child at middle school), therefore their influences must be targeted. These are middle school teachers and the local community.

Promotion

Target is to recruit 63% of siblings per annum.
Objectives are:

1 Increase parental awareness of benefits of the school.
2 Inform parents of academic successes and abilities of teaching staff.
3 Remind parents of the facilities and opportunities offered by the school.

Methods

1 Personal selling by all staff. Most effective method; needs training.
2 Advertising via weekly newsletter and other in-house magazines, encouraging Parents' Association.
3 Exhibitions.
4 Direct mail; follow up to Parents' Meetings.
5 Market research.
6 Publicity; PR.

Market segment (2)

'First time buyers' i.e. parents who have no child at the school. This group requires considerable information via literature, visits, word of mouth.

Methods

1 PR: joint ventures with middle schools – involve parents and teachers. Entrance dual use by such groups. Improve business links to confirm that the school has active interest in the future of its pupils.
2 Advertising: mail shots before Open Evening. More invitations to middle schools.
3 Market research.
4 Staff development: ensure all teachers understand the changes that are happening.

Conclusions

1 The main competitor across all age groups is School *X*, but among potential pupils it is School *Y*.
2 The school must build up its contacts with the middle schools, local businesses and the press.
3 'The School is in an exciting stage of its development. The environment in which it operates is changing and the School is facing a major threat. It is also faced with a major opportunity which its competitors do not yet appear to have grasped. The school has perceived the need

to adopt a marketing approach in order to survive. Provided the impetus is maintained and permeates all levels of the organisation there is every reason to believe that this School will emerge as an excellent school for other schools to emulate'.

Points to emerge:

1 71 per cent of respondents could not identify good or bad points of local schools.
2 Over 50 per cent give academic results as the major choice factor.
3 First choice of all respondents was School Z; this school second. Of second place choices School X is first, this school second. From 8–11 year olds, this school is third.

[*Note*: Statistical tables on which much of this data is based are not included in the resume, and are therefore not reproduced here].

Key points

1 The marketing plan begins by clearly specifying goals (short-term ends) and objectives (long-term ends), both of which are, in contrast to mission statements, quantifiable and measurable.
2 To take stock of the school's situation in terms of internal organization and competitive position, a SWOT analysis is undertaken.
3 SWOT analysis draws attention to gaps in the school's market intelligence.
4 The marketing plan highlights strategies, i.e. the means of realizing the set objectives, and specifies methods by which strategies are implemented, i.e. actual marketing activities to be undertaken, such as personal selling, advertising, exhibitions, direct mail and PR.

14

Case Study 2: Stour Valley Community School Creates a New Logo

Introduction

Nestling on the outer perimeter of a picturesque Cotswold town of Shipston-on-Stour, Warwickshire, is the local secondary school. Stour Valley Community School had, until very recently, suffered unjustifiably from a poor reputation. The introduction and promotion of a new logo – which created, among other things, a positive attitude on the part of staff, pupils and others towards the school – played a critically important part in transforming its public image into that of a worthy and respected local institution. By relating a recent marketing activity of Stour Valley School, this case study illustrates the methods by which a logo is constructed and the benefits which accrue from it.

Impetus for Designing New Logo

When the new Head Teacher of Stour Valley took office, he identified two key problems with the school's external image: it was perceived as having lacklustre leadership and unruly pupils, with all the attendant problems. With a brief from the LEA to reverse the school's decline in one year, the Head sought political support and subsequent approval to change the institution's name. In a quest to encourage Stour Valley residents to view the school as 'theirs', it was considered appropriate to include 'community' in the title. A second element in the Head's strategy involved replacing the school's logo or corporate symbol with one that seemed modern, more meaningful, and would encapsulate and express the school's *raison d'être*. The new logo had to visually articulate a corporate philosophy with which all staff, pupils and community could relate. Moreover, it had to form a focal point for all subsequent marketing and PR activities.

The school's original corporate symbol was based on the County Council's historic logo: the silhouetted figure of a bear in chains. The symbol was meaningless to most pupils, and had no obvious connection with the school or the community it served. It was patently serving no practical purpose.

Under the head's direction, children and staff participated in the creation of a new logo. Ideas were generated and screened from which a number of appropriate themes emerged: sheep, education, children, countryside, valley and river. From this list, many children had expressed overriding preference for something connected with animals. Hence, an obvious candidate for the epicentre of the logo was a sheep. Taking cognizance of this choice, it was decided that a ram would better reflect the notion of a leader; it was, after all, the first community school in the county! And for a fee of £200, a local design firm was commissioned to undertake the artwork.

The new logo now adorns every public manifestation of Stour Valley Community School: uniform, letter heads, exercise books, and all external and internal signage.

Conclusion

Thus, the school had successfully created a distinctive, simple and attractive logo which staff, pupils and community could readily associate with their organization. And it also underpinned the school's marketing and PR strategies: it provided a new, clear focus for all promotion activity; showed community and governors that something was happening, i.e. convey an image of a relatively dynamic institution; and gave staff confidence in the new Head by demonstrating that he could make things happen.

Key points

1 In order to correct its public image, the school successfully transformed its corporate identity by changing name and logo.

2 Pupils and staff were encouraged to actively participate in determining content and design of new logo.
3 The new logo is evident on school uniform, letter heads, exercise books, and all external and internal signage.
4 The new logo derived its effectiveness from

- distinctiveness
- simplicity
- attractiveness
- relevance

5 The new logo also formed a focal point for the school's marketing and PR activities.

15

Case Study 3: Competing for Sixth Form Pupils

Introduction

Notwithstanding excellent examination results, the town's local technical college suffered an unfavourable image: its portfolio of largely vocational courses had given it an inglorious status among many residents. By contrast, the college's principal rival, a grammar-school-type sixth form centre, enjoyed an esteemed reputation solely by virtue of its more traditional, academic programmes of study.

Marketing Strategy

In order to ameliorate its poor image, the college decided it would organize an open day/evening as close as possible in time to a similar event planned by the sixth form centre. Thus, visitors to both institutions would be induced to make more objective comparisons between them, the outcome of which the college confidently predicted would be to its advantage.

Marketing Activities and Methods

With its open day scheduled to occur within a few days of the sixth form centre's, letters advertising the college's event were distributed by hand to target audiences: careers officers, teachers and fifth formers from local secondary schools, selected residents and editors of local newspapers. Apart from a small press release in the local newspaper, no other advertising had been contemplated for fear it might attract visitors outside the selected target group. Additionally, senior staff designed and prepared relevant promotional material such as printed invitations, leaflets and display stands.

Elements of College Open Day

The exhibition was comprised of four key features: open day theme and supporting logo, creation of comprehensive database, display stands in foyer ('shop window' of the college's offerings), and specialist subject exhibits in appropriate classrooms and laboratories.

Logo

The open day's theme, 'Road to Success', formed the basis of a specially designed logo which provided uniform and consistent visual identity for all promotional and illustrative material.

Database

It had been intended that, as visitors entered the college building, their names, addresses and, for prospective students, intended career choices, too, would be entered in a database. This would generate a vital mailing list of potential clients to whom follow-up material could be sent. Also, it provided a basis for measuring the effectiveness of the open day as a promotional tool.

Foyer display

Having entered the college and given their details to students responsible for compiling the database, visitors were directed to the main foyer where general information about courses and careers were displayed. Here, content and layout of each display stand had been carefully composed in order to highlight the benefits which accrued to its students.

The format for all displays was, moving from top to bottom of panel:

- course title and qualification
- entry qualifications
- brief outline of course content
- photographs of the present students and their career aspirations
- a 'where are they now?' statement describing career successes of alumni

Exhibit 15.1 shows a display stand from the college exhibition, where the above format is clearly followed. Note also, the directional signage and theme logo 'Road to Success' on right side of display panel; this visual identity adorned all promotional and illustrative material.

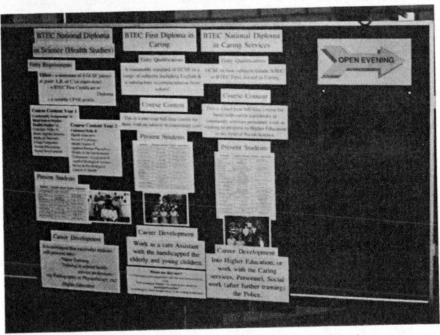

Exhibit 15.1 Exhibition display stand: 'Road to Success'

Specialist subject rooms and 'personal selling'

Having viewed the initial displays in the main foyer, visitors were directed to a number of specified subject rooms, one for each course shown on the display boards. Here, specialist staff and a sample of existing students waited to answer visitors' questions in more detail. This offered opportunities for the college to promote key selling points:

- friendliness and helpfulness of staff
- personableness, brightness and enthusiasm of students (principal PR agents for College)
- highly sophisticated technical and computer equipment used as teaching and learning aids

Critical Appraisal

Ostensibly, the open day proved a resounding success: approximately 1,000 people attended, the bulk of the estimated universe of the target audience; and it provided an inestimable opportunity for parents and their offspring to witness first hand the quality of the college's product. Some fovourable media coverage had been secured, too.

Subsequent close appraisal of the open day, however, found it wanting in a number of major particulars:

- failure to build comprehensive database
- lack of effective coordination and management of marketing activities
- college 'ambassadors' – the students – poorly briefed
- display stands appeared 'cluttered'
- inadequate control over publicity

Failure to build database

A number of students were given responsibility for noting relevant details of all visitors as they entered the college foyer. This proved unexpectedly time-consuming, leading to considerable delay and congestion in entrance hall. To facilitate easier access, the students, on their own initiative, directed visitors past the database recording point, taking details only from some of them. Hence, names, addresses and other relevant information of the vast majority of visitors eluded the database. A major opportunity had been lost to:

- identify prospective students in order to send follow-up mail shot reminding them of the college's service and for the purpose of collecting valuable marketing research material (see chapter 5)
- provide data for a before and after survey to test the effectiveness of the open day as a marketing tool, i.e. to ascertain how many open day visitors actually enrolled (see chapter 5)

Lack of effective coordination and management

Little central coordination was evident, resulting in each department 'doing its own thing', with the attendant damaging inter-departmental rivalry, duplication of publicity materials, and a lack of uniformity in presentation and quality of publicity and promotional materials. In short, senior management had neglected to ensure that the college's internal communication had been effective and appropriate for marketing (see chapter 4).

Poorly briefed participants

Many staff and students involved in the open day had received scant training for their respective roles in the event. Thus a number of critically important marketing tasks, such as compiling a comprehensive database of visitors, were left to the untutored discretion of participants. Consequently, some of these key activities had been neglected.

Cluttered display stands

While the quality of visual displays had been impressive, some of them carried too much information and consequently appeared disordered. Theoretically, stands located in the foyer served to promote general awareness of the benefits which accrued from enrolling at the college, more detailed information about these matters being available where staff might undertake personal selling. Hence, over-concentration of data on a number of display stands may have proved counter-productive. Indeed, the college seems to have been mindful of the theory: it had intended that specialist subject rooms, not display stands, should be used exclusively for disseminating details about its offerings. Evidently, an oversight on the part of the college's senior staff.

Inadequate control of publicity

Representatives from the local press had been invited to the open day. Seemingly motivated by the adage 'all publicity is good publicity', the college's senior management had granted reporters almost unfettered access in their coverage of the event. A manifestation of this policy is the article which appeared in the town's *Evening News* on 1 February: while illustrating two positive aspects of work in the college's department of science and mathematics (i.e. pictures to left and centre of photograph), a story captioned 'Making no bones about their course', seemed to trivialize. A number of staff members expressed disquiet about this publicity, arguing that it did little to promote the college's image as a serious rival to the town's coveted sixth form centre. Indeed, it would appear that this instance of media coverage had been close to the dangerous end of the publicity scale (discussed in chapter 9).

Key points

1 The college's marketing strategy involved holding an open day/evening close in time to a similar event planned by the sixth form centre.
2 The college's open day theme, 'Road to Success', formed the focal point for its marketing strategy and permeated all relevant activities.
3 The college had intended recording the names and addresses of all visitors for the purpose of building a comprehensive database of potential users of its service.
4 High quality display stands – the college's 'shop window' – formed a key element in its promotion activity.
5 A number of specialist subject rooms were used to undertake personal selling.
6 A post-open day appraisal revealed some success: the event attracted approximately 1,000 visitors.

16
Marketing Schools and Codes of Professional Practice

Education has too much come to be seen primarily as a commodity in the market place. Its human products exist not to serve God but rather the Gross National Product, and its content is judged increasingly in terms of economic utility – education as a means to an end rather than an end to itself. We end up with minds as sharp as razors and about as broad.[1]

Introduction

Marketing, it seems, is anathema to many schools. Those who object to it, do so on two counts. First, owing to its perceived association with aggressive competitiveness, marketing is considered incompatible with the profession's ethical standards. A recent newspaper report highlights this concern: 'Birmingham and Solihull teachers are set for a head-on clash over allegations that top pupils are being poached from the city . . . Birmingham union chiefs fear their neighbours are bringing back banished selection tests to draw high-achievers from the boarder areas'.[2] Critics of marketing argue that, if a school acquires a competitive edge in the market, it is likely to achieve this at another's expense. The National Association of Head Teachers (NAHT) warns that for 'every school which "wins" in a competitive market others lose and as a result the chances of their pupils will be damaged'.[3] The universe of prospective pupils that make up the market for schools is relatively finite. This contrasts with, for example, further and higher education, where hitherto largely untapped prospects (such as mature students or those without formal academic qualifications) can be successfully targeted.

Second, many senior members of the teaching profession and others such as Dr Robert Runcie maintain that education, because it is an activity of prophetic and intrinsic importance, transcends commercial considerations with which marketing is seemingly closely linked.

Evolution of Marketing in Schools

Notwithstanding these expressed reservations, marketing is practised more widely than is apparently realized. The NAHT observes that it 'is important that schools recognise that many of their existing activities are in fact marketing. These will have come into being as they have tried to be more responsive and to give public recognition to their achievements'.[4] Moreover, an increasing number of head teachers appear able to either reconcile professionalism and marketing, or accede, albeit reluctantly, that marketing is inextricably linked to their respective institution's survival. The NAHT argues:

> Schools can no longer operate in isolation. The expectations of society, whether expressed by individual parents, identifiable groups or government legislation mean that schools need to be aware of the views being expressed. They must take account of the public perceptions of how well they are performing and be prepared to respond to those articulated concerns which are genuinely representative. Marketing is about this kind of responsiveness just as much as it is about a responsibility to lead and educate the public view.[5]

A further impetus toward marketing derives from increased competition for pupils. Owing to a marked decline in birth rate over several decades, the market in which schools operate is a diminishing one. This competitive situation is aggravated by two further developments. Following recent education reforms, parents enjoy increased opportunities to 'buy' or opt for schools of their choice. In choosing, parents are likely to take account of, among other things, examination results (SAT results, public examinations, proposed league tables, etc.) which will, according to Mick Carney 'become the advertising copy of the publications department's glossy brochure, which is the main tool to support the marketing function'.[6] And the introduction of 'open enrolment' which largely determines a school's income based on number of pupils enrolled, suggests greater use will be made of marketing in a quest to maximize pupil intake.

Codes of Conduct

Evidently, if schools are to survive and respond effectively to increased competition for both resources and pupils, the use of marketing in education seems inevitable. But adherence to the highest standards of professional practice in the use of the various marketing techniques is vital if the activity is to benefit schools and win approval. In order to promote best practice in the use of marketing in schools, indicative codes of conduct covering three relevant aspects of the subject are outlined below: *general marketing behaviour, sponsorship* and *advertising*.

Code of Practice 1: General marketing behaviour

In a quest to retain public confidence in the profession, constrain the worst excesses of marketing (fearing that schools might 'promote themselves by criticising others') and 'help members to meet the challenge to market their schools',[7] the NAHT recently formulated a Code of Conduct. The Code states that, when undertaking marketing, members should:

- report results and achievements in an accurate, fair and balanced manner
- set any marketing expenditure at levels which are designed not to disadvantage present pupils
- avoid comparisons or statements which denigrate other educational establishments
- encourage the adoption of a joint policy between neighbouring schools on marketing and recruitment of pupils
- avoid the practice of giving gifts or commercial incentives to prospective pupils or their parents with the intention of inducing them to enrol
- take account of the possible damage to pupils in other educational establishments as a result of marketing activities[8]

Obviously, the effectiveness of the general code of conduct will depend on the willingness of schools to voluntarily adhere to it: in the absence of any legal sanction to enforce compliance, the NAHT proceeded on the basis that 'members are people of integrity and good sense who would be aware of the professional damage that could be caused by inappropriate marketing strategies'.

Code of Practice 2: Sponsorship

Equally important is the establishment of principles relating to sponsorship since some parents, it seems, have reservations about this aspect of marketing. Ian Spero, managing director of sponsorship consultancy Spero Communications, articulates this concern: 'I have a five-year-old son. I would object quite strongly to him coming home with an exercise book with a brand on it. Children are influenced from a multitude of sources and schools have a responsibility to protect children.'[9] And Spero's views are not without foundation: the National Consumer Council recently discovered that industrial sponsorship in schools had resulted in over half the sponsored school books, teaching packs and videos contained promotional bias and inaccuracies.

Though the National Consumer Council has drawn up guidelines on sponsorship, hitherto, no explicit code of conduct has existed covering this aspect of school marketing. In response to pressure from schools in its authority, however, Solihull Metropolitan Borough Council's Education Sub-Committee, following an initiative of its Director of Education, recently published a formalized code of conduct for sponsorship. The code, which offers practical guidance for all schools concerned about sponsorship, reads as follows:

The appropriateness of any form of sponsorship to the school should be considered very carefully to avoid any compromise of the reputation of the school or the Local Education Authority.

There should be demonstrable education/financial benefit to the school with no strings attached.

Written advance confirmation from the potential sponsors of their expectations of the school in return for their sponsorship.

All offers of sponsorship to be considered by the Governors, together with the conditions of sponsorship.

Acknowledgement of external sponsorship to be discreet, e.g. on school brochures, the acknowledgement of sponsorship to occupy a small space on the cover or flyleaf. Similarly, any *logo* on donated sports vests and similar to be discreet and of relatively smaller size to the school name.

Parents to be informed of sponsorship and, wherever possible, its objectives to be stated clearly.

The financial benefit to the school of a sponsor to be shown clearly in the school's audited accounts.

Where there is any uncertainty over the wisdom of a form of sponsorship, the matter should be raised with the Director of Education.

The form of any sponsorship agreement to be agreed by the Director of Education and/or the Town Clerk.[10]

Code of Practice 3: Advertising

Another manifest concern of many teachers relates to advertising. In general, it is desirable that advertisments adhere to the principles advocated by organisations such as the Advertising Standards Authority. Here, is it demanded that advertising is

- legal
- decent
- honest
- truthful

Doubtless all schools will countenance the above general guidelines in their advertising, but the Section 'Code of Conduct 1' above lists a number of generic ethical principles which are more specific in their application to schools. Namely:

- advertising examination results must be 'accurate, fair and balanced'
- use of school resources for advertising should not 'disadvantage present pupils'
- advertisements must not make comparisons which 'denigrate other educational establishments'

Education services are, to varying degrees, protected from the excesses of promotion activity by both statutory and voluntary controls.[11] The 1989 Education (School Management) Regulations, for example, control important aspects of advertising (and covers sponsorship, too). But teachers themselves are assiduous arbiters of advertising in their schools and are likely to prove a prime source of voluntary control over promotion intemperance. As the Head Teacher of Highstead Grammar School for Girls in Kent, discovered when she sold advertising space on school premises: 'The scheme was not awfully popular with staff; I had to explain on my hands and knees that the money would be useful.' Perhaps this explains the National Consumer Council's confidence in the profession's propriety and capacity for self-regulation when it asked teachers to ensure that sponsored and advertising material in schools is 'acceptable'.

Key points

1 Notwithstanding ethical objections to marketing education, circumstances dictate its inevitable use by schools if they are to survive.
2 In view of the inevitability of marketing in schools, a number of codes of conduct have been designed to maintain the highest standards of professional practice and promote the acceptability of the activity in education.
3 Only by strict adherence by schools to specified codes of conduct will marketing gain acceptance by teachers, parents and the community.
4 Codes of professional practice relate to three specific areas of activity: general marketing behaviour (See 'Code of Practice 1'), sponsorship (See 'Code of Practice 2') and advertising (See 'Code of Practice 3').
5 Code of Practice 1 emphasizes honesty, fairness, refraining from denigrating rival schools, joint/group/collaborative marketing, and desisting from offering promotional items.
6 Code of Practice 2 stresses the need for schools to be circumspect in accepting sponsorship from external bodies, to resist entering into any commitment with a sponsor, to ensure governors are responsible for decisions relating to sponsorship, and to be clear as to the benefits that accrue from sponsorship.
7 Code of Practice 3 demands that generally all advertising by schools is legal, decent, honest and truthful. More specifically, it urges that advertising by schools is accurate, fair and balanced, does not absorb resources to the detriment of teaching and pupils' interests, and does not denigrate rival schools.

Notes

1 Dr Robert Runcie, speaking at the Headmasters' Conference, 1990. Quoted by Donald MacLeod, 'State Should Help Pay Boarding School Fees', *Independent*, 19 September 1990.
2 Fay Gould, 'Schools Accused of Pupil Poaching', *Birmingham Daily News*, 8 March 1990.
3 National Association of Head Teachers (NAHT), *The Marketing of Schools* (Council Memorandum), National Association of Head Teachers, September 1990, para. 3.4.
4 Ibid., para. 3.3.
5 Ibid., para. 3.13.
6 Quoted in the *Guardian*, 17 April 1990.
7 NAHT, *Marketing*, para. 1.2.
8 Ibid., para. 1.1; see also correspondence between the Author and Education Management Information Exchange, Slough, Berks, UK, during 1990. The launch of the National Association of Head Teachers' Code of Conduct received extensive publicity: see 'Heads Warned Off Poaching Pupils with "Freebie" Bait', *Observer*, 9 September 1990; 'Heads Order Ban on Gifts Intended to Attract More Pupils', *The Times*, 10 September 1990; 'Code of Conduct to Curb Schools' Recruiting Ploys', *Daily Telegraph*, 10 September 1990.
9 A. Quassim, 'Surviving on a Private Income', *Marketing Week*, vol. 13, no. 29, 28 September 1990, p. 42.
10 Solihull Metropolitan Borough Council, Education Sub-Committee, Minutes of Meeting, Item 5, 'Sponsorship of Schools', 22 May 1990.
11 Advertising is strictly regulated by a number of instruments of control which apply also to schools. These controls are either statutory or voluntary. The Trade Description Acts of 1968 and 1972 (Part III), the Consumer Protection Act 1987, which amends to the 1968 and 1972 Acts, and the Fair Trading Act 1973, have been effective in maintaining reasonably high standards of honesty in advertising. In the case of voluntary controls, this has been achieved to a reasonably impressive degree by advertisers themselves. In 1961, the British Code of Advertising Practice, for example, established 'rules' governing all print and screen advertisments. And similar codes of

practice complement the process of voluntary control. To police the advertisers' behaviour in the UK, the Advertising Standards Authority, though lacking executive power, has proved a formidable body in ensuring that all advertisments not covered by statutory controls are legal, decent, honest and truthful.

17

Conclusion: Performance Evaluation

What it [British Standards Award] enables [a school] to do is to provide an assurance to its customers, whether they be the pupils, parents, guardians, or local education authorities, that it has a systematic way of going about its business.[1]

Controlling and Monitoring the School's Marketing Activities

Successful marketing of schools involves assiduous management of all relevant activities and processes. Those responsible for initiating and implementing the school's marketing campaign, usually the head and other senior staff or specially convened team, should endeavour to control and monitor every key aspect of the marketing programme. Some of the organizational features which are essential to this undertaking were covered in chapter 4, where the process of internal communication is outlined, and chapters 8 and 9 which emphasize the importance of control and monitoring of image building and PR activities.

A statement of progress in the implementation of the various marketing activities and identification of attendant problems should be communicated regularly to all staff, and, where relevant, pupils, too. In this way, as emphasized in chapter 4, the school community will feel more involved and committed to the success of the school's marketing endeavours.

Earlier, methods for appraising the effectiveness of specific marketing activities, such as open days, press releases, individual advertisments, logos and other corporate signage and exhibitions, were discussed. Important though these methods are, it is essential also to ascertain the contribution of each marketing activity to outcome. For example: where a school determines to increase the number of applicants for places, and where its advertising campaign is intended to accomplish this objective, it is possible that any enhancement to its popularity may be attributable to an unforeseen event, such as rival institutions suffering adverse publicity. As far as practicable, it is essential to establish the degree of causal connection or linkage between each discrete marketing tool used by the school and the realization of individual campaign objectives. Some of the survey methods and questionnaire exercises discussed in chapter 5 and illustrated in the appendices, will help pin-point the precise contribution of individual marketing activities to the realization of the school's marketing objectives.

While activities such as these are important, a comprehensive appraisal of the whole of the marketing effort – a corporate perspective or overview – must be undertaken at a later stage in the marketing implementation process, perhaps after three complete terms (see chapter 3, figures 3.1 and 3.2). In order to achieve this objective, and to devise appropriate corrective measures, it is necessary to undertake a:

> *comprehensive, systematic, independent,* and *periodic* examination of an institution's marketing environment, objectives, strategies, and activities with a view to determine problem areas and opportunities and recommending a plan of action to improve the institution's marketing performance.[2]

Quality

So far, the emphasis has been on measuring marketing performance. This does not, however, reveal the quality of education provided.[3] What, then, is quality is education provision? And how might it be obtained?

Though a complex and difficult concept to define, three discrete but interconnected criteria for evaluating quality in education, are commonly used:[4]

- the degree to which an education product satisfies the wants of consumers (pupils) and customers (parents and others)

- differences in the quantity of some desired tangible attribute or feature of the education product or school
- conformance to recognized education standards

The first definition echoes the thoughts of Wilma Mathews who suggests quality 'is what the customer says it is'.[5] Indeed, this is reminiscent of parental demands for a number of educational features which they frequently associate with good schools: 'outstanding examination results', 'smaller classes', 'better teachers', 'superior facilities', 'school uniforms', 'high standards of pupil behaviour', and so on. In this context, quality is largely subjective and often difficult to measure,[6] as Francis Beckett points out in connection with the issue of better teachers: 'Quality of teaching . . . is not easily judged. A teacher is not like a sales representative, who can be simply judged on sales figures'.[7]

The second definition of quality relates to tangible constituents of the education product, such as libraries and science laboratories and similar physical entities of the kind described in chapter 7. Where a school provides these attributes in sufficiently large quantities (i.e. well-stocked library and ample laboratory facilities), it may be considered to offer a quality product to that extent at least. In contrast to the first definition of the concept, here quality is quantifiable and therefore more easily measurable.[8]

The third definition refers to independent measures of education performance, such as HMI quality ratings and examination results. Though questionable as a fair basis for comparing schools, published league tables of schools' examination performance (where 'added value' is included) might be used to determine quality in the foreseeable future.

These definitions are all 'part of a comprehensive approach to improving quality'.[9] When used in a complementary manner (none is sufficiently reliable on its own), supplemented by reference to the list of attributes shown in chapter 3 (see pp. 19-21), these criteria provide a basis for measuring quality in education performance and product offering.

According to one head, 'success is built up gradually by excellent staff and good facilities – if these are right, there is no need for the hard-sell. Quality always sells itself'.[10] Wilma Mathews offers more specific guidance: a prerequisite for quality is an organization's capacity and wherewithal for critical and honest self-appraisal, and a willingness on its part to become self-aware and responsive. Evidently, the effectiveness of a school's internal and external communication (as discussed in chapters 4, 8, 9 and 10), will determine its capacity to provide quality: 'Most experts admit', Mathews proclaims, 'that quality itself is 90 per cent the result of good communication . . . [it] plays a vital role in achieving quality for any organisation . . . [it must] show that it isn't afraid to measure itself'.[11]

Success in providing quality education depends also on establishing organizational mechanisms for *continually monitoring the service offered* at every level or point in the delivery process (see earlier section in this chapter): 'we can't wait until the end of the line to have someone tell us it won't work'.[12] Moreover, in attempting to introduce a type of 'total quality control' into the school, all staff must be actively involved in the process of continually searching for and correcting shortfalls in quality service.[13]

Conclusion

The acronym, SOAR, highlights key features of school marketing covered in the book and represents a sound basis for achieving success:

SOLICIT your consumers' (children's) and customers' (parent's) ideas
OPEN the internal and external communication flow
ACT on what you hear, good and bad
REWARD the behaviour of clients and staff who hear and share your
   customers' comments[14]

This book has emphasized continually the need for the utmost circumspection and sensitivity in marketing. It has stressed also that a school's expectation of the contribution of marketing to its future success must be realistic: a principal purpose of the activity is to assist schools to design relevant quality products and to help them tell selected target audiences about their offerings. Marketing is not a panacea for inadequate educational provision or bad schools. In this context, Peter Downes's advice seems singularly apt:

> the best sales pitch for the product of a school is the satisfaction
> of the pupils and the parents. And if you are doing a good job, if
> your staff are teaching well, if there is a good extra curricular life,
> if the pastoral system is effective, if children actually enjoy being

there and the teachers enjoy being there, then that is the best marketing of all, and no amount of glossies will mask inefficiencies and inadequacies in the basic schooling.[15]

Key points

1 Those staff members responsible for initiating and implementing the school's marketing campaign should endeavour to *control* and *monitor* every key aspect of the marketing programme.
2 As far as practicable, it is essential to establish the degree of causal connection or linkage between each marketing tool used by the school and the realization of individual campaign objectives.
3 Additionally, a comprehensive appraisal of the whole of the marketing effort must be undertaken at a later stage in the marketing implementation process.
4 There are three possible criteria for evaluating quality in education:

   ● the degree to which an education product satisfies the wants of consumers and customers
   ● differences in the quantity of some desired tangible attribute or feature of the education product or school
   ● conformance to recognized education standards

5 All three criteria should be used together, plus an additional criterion which is used in connection with the SWOT analysis, to assess a school's quality rating.
6 Achieving quality in education involves establishing effective internal and external methods of communication.
7 The acronym SOAR, represents sound advice for achieving success in school marketing.

Notes

1 Stephen Dewhurst, British Standards Institute, talking about Kates Hill County Primary School, Dudley, West Midlands. BBC 1, *Regional News*, 13 January 1992.
2 Philip Kotler & Karen F. A. Fox, *Strategic Marketing for Educational Institutions*, Prentice-Hall, USA, 1985, p. 384.
3 Ibid., p. 385.

4 D. A. Garvin, 'What Does "Product Quality" Really Mean?', *Sloan Management Review*, vol. 25, no. 1, Autumn, 1984; also quoted in E. R. Gray and I. Smeltzer, *Management: the competitive edge*, Macmillan, New York, 1989.

5 Wilma Mathews, manager of PR at AT&T Network Systems, quoted in *Communication Briefings*, vol. 8, no. 2, 1989, Pitman, NY.

6 See E. R. Gray and L. R. Smeltzer, *Management*, p. 748.

7 Francis Beckett, 'The schools that *must* do better', *The Independent*, 15 November 1990.

8 Ibid.

9 E. R. Gray and L. R. Smeltzer, *Management*, p. 749.

10 Independent School Survey Results, Appendix A: Survey into School Marketing.

11 Wilma Mathews, quoted in *Communication Briefings*.

12 Ibid.

13 Gray and Smeltzer, *Management*, p. 750.

14 George Walther, cited in *Delaware Valley Eagle*, Delaware Valley Business Forms Inc., P.O. Box 5017, Cherry Hill, NJ 08034.

15 P. Downes and M. Hopkinson, *Managing Education in the 1990s – Local Management in Practice*, The Chartered Institute of Public Finance and Accountancy, London, 1989, pp. 12–13.

Appendix A:
Survey into School Marketing

Introduction

Between late autumn 1989 and early spring 1990 the author undertook a survey into marketing in schools. Questionnaires were distributed to a representative sample of 600 independent/non-maintained sector schools. For comparative purposes, maintained sector schools within the Metropolitan Borough of Solihull, West Midlands, were also surveyed with the support of the its Education Department. Owing to a recent boundary change and other relevant developments, Solihull's LEA schools were sufficiently typical in a number of important particulars for the purpose of the survey. Accordingly, questionnaires were distributed to all 100 of the borough's maintained sector schools.

From the independent sector, 312 valid questionnaires where returned (52% return rate) and 44 completed questionnaires were received from Solihull schools (44% return rate).

Though a facsimile of the questionnaire used in the research is not included here, the questions put to respondents and a summary of the survey results, are given below.

Survey Results

Question 1   To what extent do you agree/disagree with the following statement?

'The identification of a school with a sponsor in name, style and colour of brand publicity, logo, etc., is undesirable'.

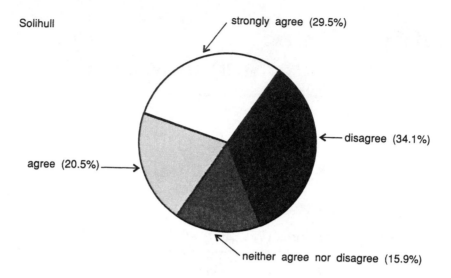

Solihull

strongly agree (29.5%)

disagree (34.1%)

agree (20.5%)

neither agree nor disagree (15.9%)

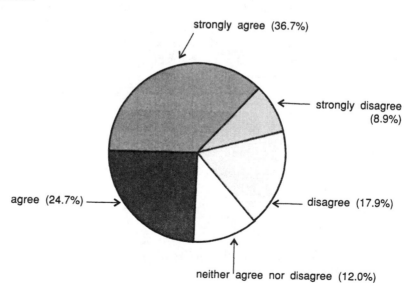

Independent

strongly agree (36.7%)

strongly disagree (8.9%)

agree (24.7%)

disagree (17.9%)

neither agree nor disagree (12.0%)

Question 2   To what extent do you associate the following activities with the concept of marketing?

Solihull

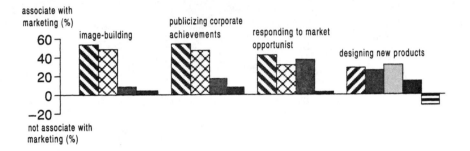

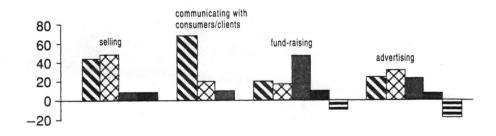

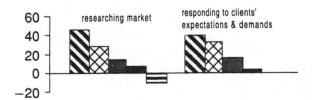

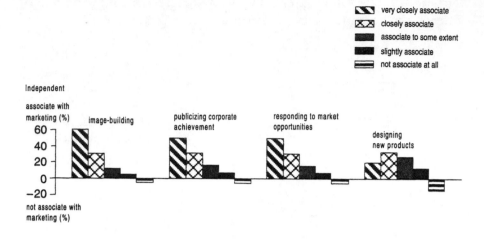

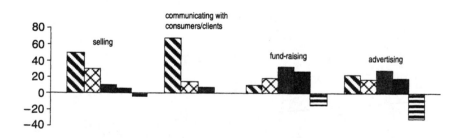

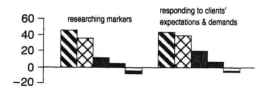

Question 3   Which category most accurately describes your school's level of experience in marketing?

Solihull

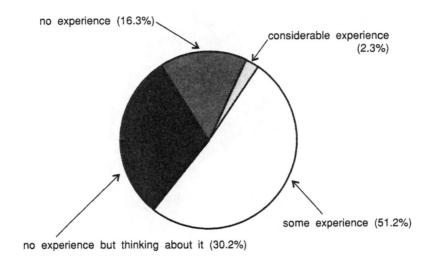

no experience (16.3%)

considerable experience (2.3%)

some experience (51.2%)

no experience but thinking about it (30.2%)

Independent

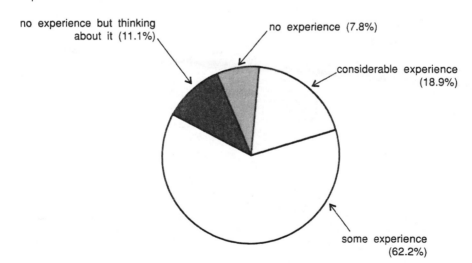

no experience but thinking about it (11.1%)

no experience (7.8%)

considerable experience (18.9%)

some experience (62.2%)

Question 4   How important/unimportant is marketing likely to be
to your school in the foreseeable future?

Solihull

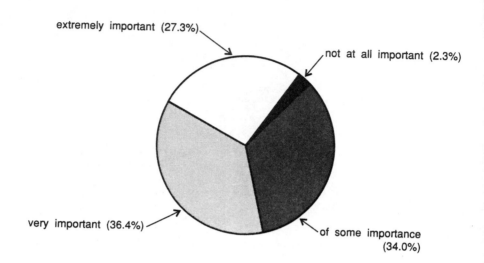

Independent

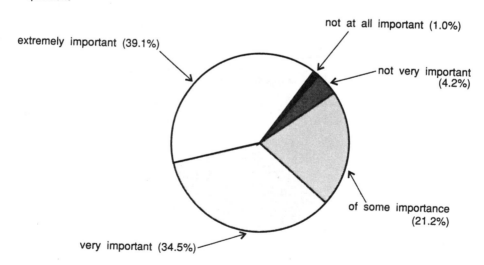

Question 5 How receptive are your staff to marketing?

Solihull

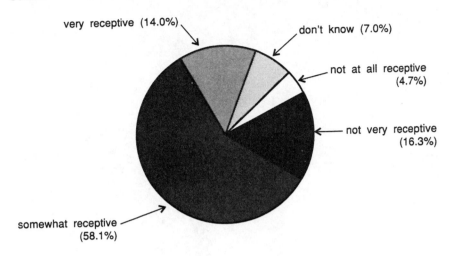

very receptive (14.0%)

don't know (7.0%)

not at all receptive
(4.7%)

not very receptive
(16.3%)

somewhat receptive
(58.1%)

Independent

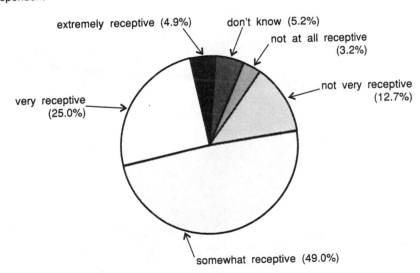

extremely receptive (4.9%)

don't know (5.2%)

not at all receptive
(3.2%)

not very receptive
(12.7%)

very receptive
(25.0%)

somewhat receptive (49.0%)

Question 6   Using the scale below, how would you categorize your school's style of management?

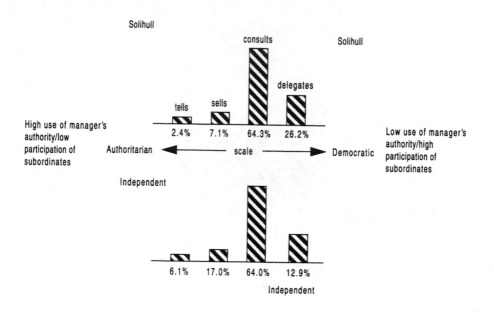

Question 7   At what stage, if any, is your school in the marketing process?

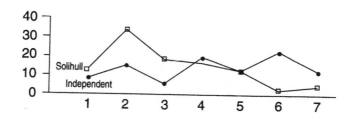

Stages
1 not contemplating marketing school
2 thinking about marketing
3 establishing marketing team
4 undertaking review
5 setting objectives, selecting strategies
6 implementing strategies
7 monitoring & reviewing strategies

Question 8 If your school is between stages (2) and (7) above, which staff have been most closely involved in this process?

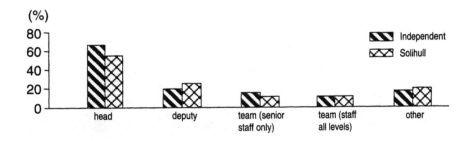

Question 9 How important/unimportant do you consider marketing to be as a means of ameliorating the following problems?

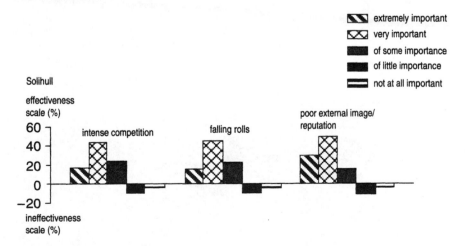

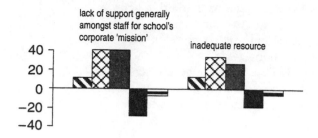

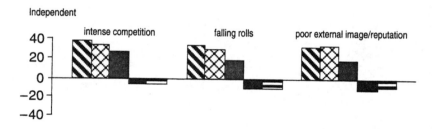

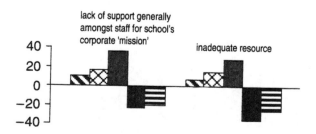

Question 10 Has your school (or agent acting on its behalf) undertaken any informal or formal market research or systematic enquiry to enhance your understanding of the changing education market?

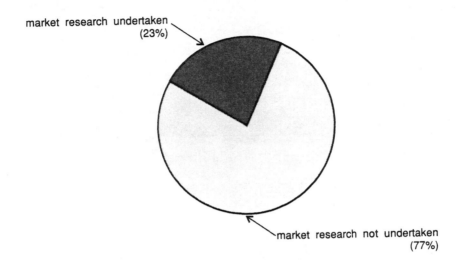

Solihull

market research undertaken (23%)

market research not undertaken (77%)

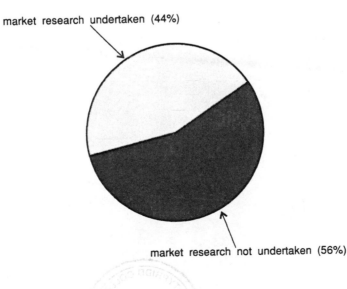

Independent

market research undertaken (44%)

market research not undertaken (56%)

Question 11   If the answer to Question 10 above is yes, which of the following methods proved most useful/least useful in providing you with further insight to your market?

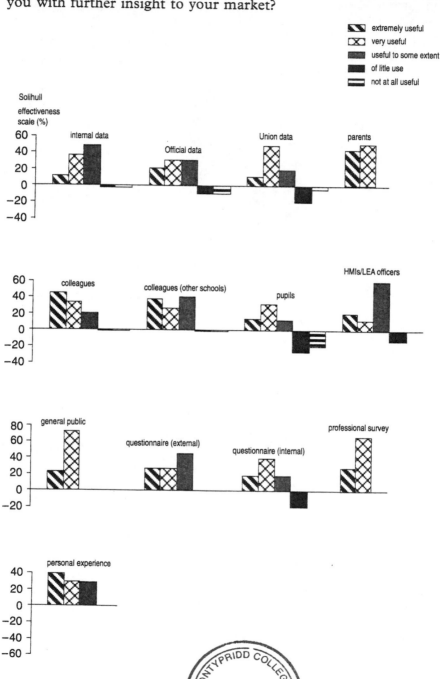

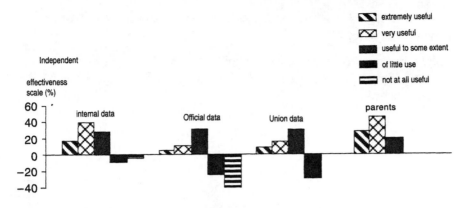

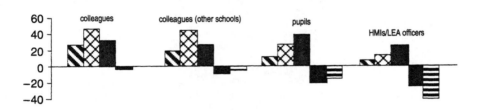

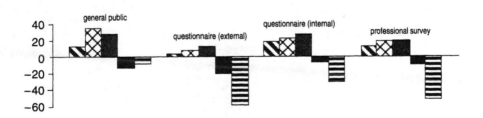

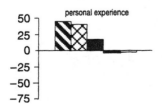

Question 12 To what extent do you agree/disagree with the following statement:

'Effective communication between head and staff and vice versa is critically important in gaining internal support for the school's corporate mission'.

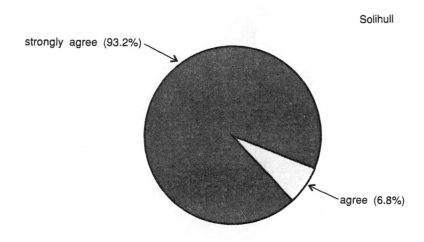

Solihull

strongly agree (93.2%)

agree (6.8%)

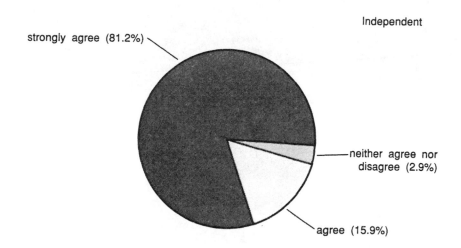

Independent

strongly agree (81.2%)

neither agree nor disagree (2.9%)

agree (15.9%)

Question 13 In your opinion, how effective/ineffective are the following channels of communication?

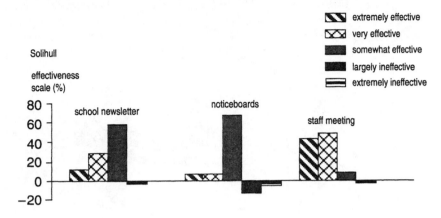

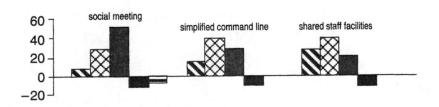

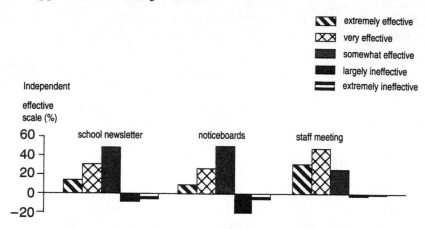

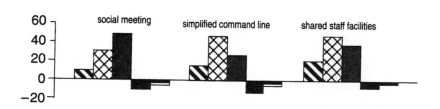

Question 14 Using the scale below, how would you rate the actual or likely reaction of your staff to marketing the school?

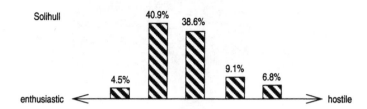

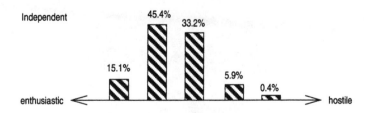

Question 15   Have you recently introduced measures to enhance
the image of your school?

Solihull

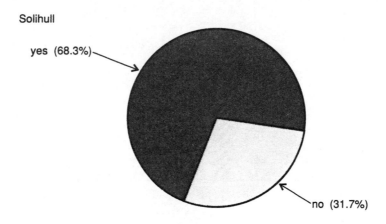

Independent

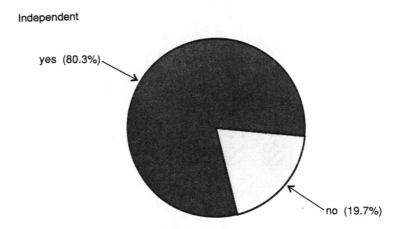

Question 16 How effective/ineffective do you consider the following image-building techniques to be?

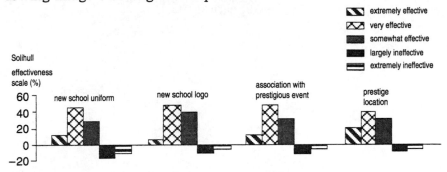

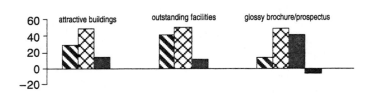

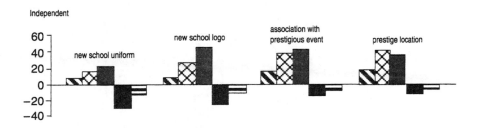

Question 17   How effective/ineffective do you think the following techniques/activities to be in targeting your message on discrete consumer segments in the education market?

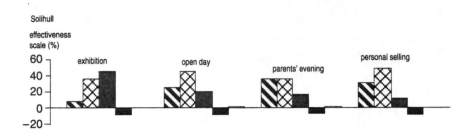

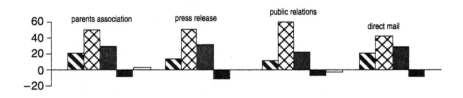

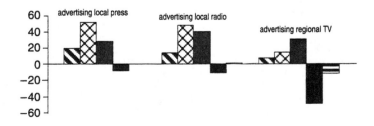

Independent

Effectiveness
scale (%)

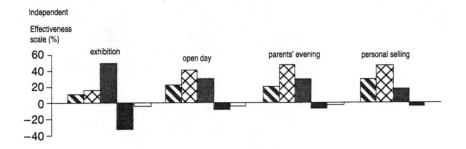

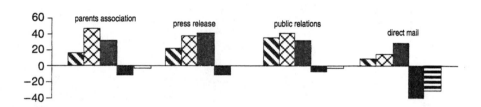

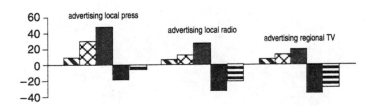

Question 18 How important do you consider the following activities/situations to be in equipping your school for effective marketing?

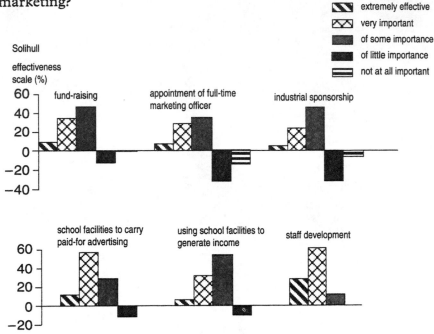

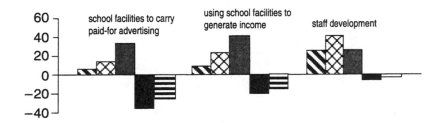

Question 19 What single factor do you think is most likely to threaten the success of your school's marketing endeavours?

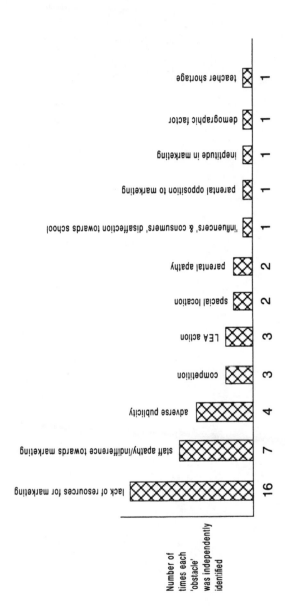

Solihull

teacher shortage 1

demographic factor 1

ineptitude in marketing 1

parental opposition to marketing 1

'influencers' & consumers' disaffection towards school 1

parental apathy 2

special location 2

LEA action 3

competition 3

adverse publicity 4

staff apathy/indifference towards marketing 7

lack of resources for marketing 16

Number of times each 'obstacle' was independently identified

Independent

Obstacle	Number of times each obstacle was independently identified
Labour Government	40
economic recession in UK	35
lack of resources for marketing	31
adverse publicity	29
ineptitude in marketing	27
competition	24
unfavourable examination results	24
'influence' & consumers' disaffection towards school	19
demographic factors	9
staff complacency	8
staff apathy/indifference towards marketing	6
price sensitivity	4
'buyer' resistance	4
spacial location	4
teacher shortage	3
low profile	3
failure to address educational isues of the day	1
moving image of school down-market	1
raising false expectation	1
'atmospherics' found wanting	1

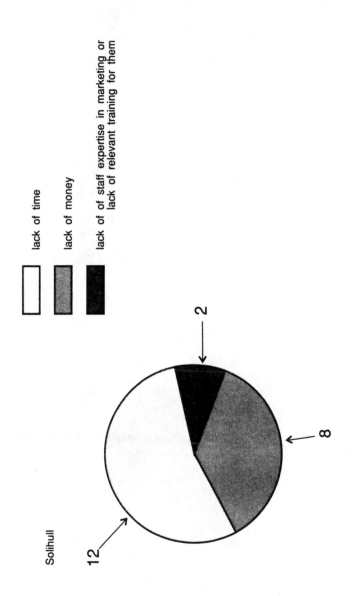

lack of time

lack of money

lack of of staff expertise in marketing or lack of relevant training for them

Solihull

12

2

8

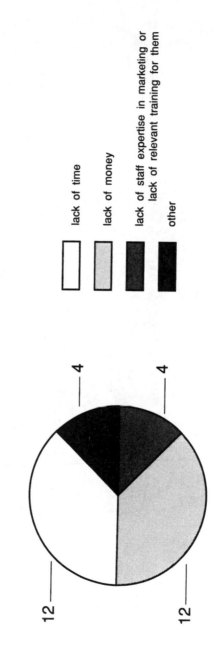

Independent

lack of time

lack of money

lack of staff expertise in marketing or
lack of relevant training for them

other

Appendix B:
Questionnaire Design

Deciding What to Include

A first step in constructing a questionnaire involves establishing clear objectives for the survey. Some key initial questions are: 'What is the questionnaire intending to find out?' and 'what sort of information is it required to elicit?' Answers to these questions will help ascertain what is needed in the questionnaire, and what is extraneous to it. This is a ruthlessly selective process: relevant questions only must be included, and the researcher must desist from including questions that do not explicitly promote the realization of the survey's objectives, irrespective of their intrinsic interest.

Types of Questionnaire

Virtually all research instruments for gathering education data involve the use of questionnaires. Evidently, the choice of technique and associated questionnaire will depend on the appraisal made in terms of the listed variables. But of relevance also is, as Boyd et al. point out,[1] the type of *information sought* and the type of *respondents* or *sample* to be used.

In undertaking a research project, a school may need to use several techniques and therefore a number of questionnaires. For example, structured interviews involving a sample of respondents being questioned in the local community where the interviewer completes the questionnaire him/herself, and the respondent subsequently takes away a self-completion questionnaire.

The level of 'perfection' needed in the construction of question-naires varies: those used for in-depth interviews, for example, demand a lower level of exactitude in their preparation than, say, postal questionnaires where the researcher cannot control, prompt or assist the respondent but must anticipate probable reactions and problems during the construction stage.

Rules for Designing a Questionnaire

In constructing a questionnaire, the researcher must

- ensure opening question is sufficiently interesting in order to motivate the respondent to complete questionnaire
- avoid personal questions, but if imperative, hide personal part in the end of the questionnaire to prevent respondent being turned off early in survey
- avoid ambiguous, complex and long questions; keep questions clear, simple and short
- ensure questions are meaningful to respondent; i.e. takes account of their experience and knowledge
- avoid leading questions
- keep length of questionnaire as short as practicable
- ensure questionnaire is user-friendly, i.e. clearly and attractively laid out, easy to complete and contains a stamped addressed envelope for return
- include covering letter in which the rationale for the survey is explained, but avoid priming respondent too much
- take account of the need to induce respondents to participate in questionnaire exercise, either by maximizing interest, offering incentives, or both

Type of Question

A key consideration in questionnaire construction is the choice and wording of questions. The form which any question takes will depend on the nature of the research, for

> there is no unique right way of asking any question, because it should be related to the purpose of the survey, and the projected way of analysing and using the data. A question which is 'right' in

one context may be unsuitable in another, and a degree of accuracy essential for one purpose may be irrelevant and wasteful for another.[2]

While a detailed exposition of the main types of questions relevant to questionnaires are provided in The Market Research Society's publication *Standard Questions*, the following is a list of some of the principal categories.

Questions can be either open or closed Open refers to questions that do not offer predetermined categories of possible answers, the respondent being free to answer in their own words. Closed questions require the respondent to select from a number of given, possible answers. Replies to open questions are usually difficult to quantify and are often located at end of questionnaire; they are frequently used for in-depth interviews (see below), only very sparingly in other situations. Conversely, closed questions form the essence of structured, postal and self-completion questionnaires.

Questions usually fall into three specific categories

> Classification of respondents, e.g.
> > How old are you?
> > (Please tick)
> > [ ] 11–16
> > [ ] 17–18
> > [ ] 19–21

> Behaviour in the product field, e.g.
> > Why did you choose this school?
> > (Please tick)
> > [ ] It was nearest to home
> > [ ] Advised to come here
> > [ ] Reputation of school
> > [ ] Extra-curricular activities

> And attitude measurement, e.g.
> > Indicate the extent to which you
> > agree/disagree with the statement that
> > small schools generally provide a
> > better education than larger schools.
> > (Please tick)
> > [ ] strongly agree
> > [ ] agree on the whole
> > [ ] neither agree nor disagree
> > [ ] disagree on the whole
> > [ ] strongly disagree

Closed questions can take a number of forms

Dichotomous

Have any members of your immediate
family attended an independent
school? (circle one)
a. No
b. Yes

Multiple choice

Who had most influence on your
choice of school? (circle one)
a. Parents
b. Friends
c. Current teacher(s)
d. Current students
e. Other

Rating scale

Please evaluate the following
admission-related activities for both
Academy and the school you named
in question 9. Use a rating of 1 (very
negative) through 5 (very positive);
enter '0' if not applicable.

Academy   Other school
(1–5)   (1–5)

a. Attention to me as an individual
b. Phone contact with admissions office
c. Correspondence with admissions office
d. Admission catalog
e. On-campus interview/tutor
f. Contact with students at the school
g. Contact with alumni/ae
h. Your overall response to admission contact
i. Your parents' overall response to admission contact

Importance scale

What level of importance would you
give to the following factors when
choosing a school?

VI I U LI NI

academic results
social & sports facilities

wide range of subjects
friendly atmosphere
discipline
time taken to travel to school

(example taken from questionnaire
shown in Appendix C)

Semantic differential

Using the bipolar scale below, indicate
the point that most closely represents
the direction and intensity of your
feelings towards the School:

academic :——:——:——:——: comprehensive
strict   :——:——:——:——: liberal
caring   :——:——:——:——: impersonal

Likert scale

Boarding schools encourage the early
development of pupils' independence

Please tick one box

strongly agree   [1]
agree   [2]
neither agree nor disagree   [3]
disagree   [4]
strongly disagree   [5]

An illustration of an open question is:

Have you any comments to make
about what the college should be doing
to get its message across?

Wording of Questions

In choosing the most apposite words for questions, the research
must be cognizant of a number of simple rules: avoid ambiguity,
desist from using leading questions, keep words simple and sentences and questions short and succinct, and desist from using
expressions that might offend the respondent.

Response Rate

It is vital that the questionnaire is of sufficient interest to the respondent to encourage and sustain their continued participation in the exercise. As a rule, the greater the intrinsic interest a respondent has in the subject of the questionnaire the higher their propensity to complete it. In an experimental survey, researchers at Sheffield University's Education Faculty found that a poorly constructed questionnaire (intentionally so designed for the purpose of the experiment), secured a return rate of nearly 90 percent owing to respondents' known keen interest in the subject matter, i.e. teachers' pay. A finely tuned, near-perfect questionnaire of conspicuously less intrinsic interest to teachers, was also distributed to relevant samples but elicited a very low return.

Ordering of Questions

While it is not always possible for the subject of a questionnaire to appeal to respondents, the opening question should endeavour to arouse their interest or curiosity sufficiently to induce them to participate in the survey. Indeed, the relevance of this initial question to the theme of the survey is subordinate to its interest value.

The order in which questions are placed must be logical and the direction of questioning comprehensible to the respondent. It is usual to begin a structured questionnaire with classification-type questions, followed by behavioural and then attitudinal questions. In the case of all but in-depth interview questionnaires, most questions are likely to be closed, with the general exception of penultimate and final questions which are usually open. Difficult or personal questions should appear late on in questionnaire in order to avoid embarrassment to respondents and thus discouraging them from completing the questions.

The effect of question sequence is also a matter of concern in constructing a questionnaire. It is well documented that most questions have influence on succeeding questions. In order to minimize the risk of bias in a respondent's answers, the most influential questions should be located late in the questionnaire.

Where questions are inserted for the purpose of testing the accuracy of respondents' replies, then relevant questions will need to be buried. Here is an illustration of this technique. In the Solihull Independent School survey, which is dealt with in Appendix A, the accuracy of Question 5 was supported by a buried question, i.e. Question 14 in the questionnaire. Both are reproduced below.

Q.5   How receptive are your staff to marketing?

Please tick

extremely receptive	[ ] 1
very receptive	[ ] 2
somewhat receptive	[ ] 3
not very receptive	[ ] 4
not at all receptive	[ ] 5
don't know	[ ] 6

Q.14   Using the scale below, how would you rate the actual or likely reaction of your staff to marketing the school?

Please indicate approximate point of scale

Enthusiastic +———+———+———+———+ Hostile
                 1   2   3   4   5

Layout

In constructing the questionnaire, consideration must be given also to physical layout and print quality. The organization must be clear, consistent, questions numbered in sequence, with even and reasonably generous spacing between questions, and good quality print finish. The size of the questionnaire is important too, especially for self-completion and postal questionnaires. Here, a convenient size is A4 or slightly smaller, or a booklet format. Generally 10 to 20 questions will suffice for most surveys. Moreover, it is helpful to include boxes or spaces where respondents can easily record their answers.

Pilot Survey

Few questionnaires are perfect, but a pilot survey conducted in near field conditions will help ameliorate the most serious shortcomings in it. The testing of a draft questionnaire usually involves interviewing a number of typical respondents to assess their reactions to individual questions, general layout, question sequence, and so on. Here, the researcher is seeking to establish whether any questions are difficult or unclear to those being interviewed. In the almost certain likelihood of the draft questionnaire being found wanting in some particular, necessary changes and modifications must be made. Depending on the severity of the changes made, a further pilot may be warranted. Then, the questionnaire is ready for use in the field.

Coding of Questions and Analysis of Findings

In order to facilitate analysis of respondents' answers it is common practice to precode questions. This involves simply numbering each possible entry against each question. The results from the completed questionnaire are then transferred to computer using the given coding numbers. Though comparatively straightforward, the exercise can be time consuming, especially where many entries to the computer are made. The software package SPSSx, which is referred to in Appendix D, can be employed to undertake necessary analysis of the data.

Notes

1 H. Boyd, S. Westfall and T. Stasch, *Marketing Research*, Unwin Inc., Chicago, 1987, p. 224.
2 Alan R. Wolfe (ed.), *Standard Questions*, The Market Research Society, London, 1984, p. 6.

Appendix C: Model Questionnaire

THE QUESTIONNAIRE

M/F

Q1 Have you any children aged between 8 and 16 attending a Sutton Coldfield school?   Y   N   END

Q1b How many children do you have between these ages?

Q1c What sex are they?

Q2 Which area do you live in?

Q3 Do you happen to know the first 3 letters of your postcode?

Q4 Are you aware which secondary schools you can send your child/children to?
                    Y   N

Q4b Can you name as many local schools as possible?

RANK

ARTHUR TERRY
FAIRFAX
PLANTSBROOK
JOHN WILLMOTT SCHOOL
BISHOP WALSH
BISHOP VESEY
SUTTON GIRLS

OTHERS

Q5 Which order or preference would you give for these schools if deciding which one to send your child to?

RANK

ARTHUR TERRY
FAIRFAX
PLANTSBROOK
JOHN WILLMOTT SCHOOL
BISHOP WALSH
BISHOP VESEY
SUTTON GIRLS

OTHERS

Q5b Why do you prefer school 1?

Q5c Why do you next prefer school 2?

Q5d Why do you least prefer school x?

Q6 What is your overall impression (image) of the following schools, if any, from the card I will now show you.

(show card A)

E VG G N P VP DK

PLANTSBROOK
FAIRFAX
ARTHUR TERRY
JOHN WILLMOTT SCHOOL
BISHOP WALSH
BISHOP VESEY
SUTTON GIRLS

Q7 Which people, if any, do you think would influence you when choosing which school to send your child to?

Q8 How important do the following factors influence your choice of school, if any?

(show card B)

VI I U LI NI

FRIENDS RECOMMENDATIONS
SCHOOL ATTENDED BY ELDER BROTHER/SISTER
YOUR OWN PREFERENCE

YOUR PARTNERS PREFERENCE
JOINT PREFERENCE
YOUR CHILDS PREFERENCE
YOUR CHILDS FRIENDS ATTENDING A CERTAIN
  SCHOOL
ARE THERE ANY OTHER POINTS?

Q9   What factors would you look for when choosing a
school for your child? (for example, 'good teachers')

Q10   What level of importance would you give to the
following factors when choosing a school?

(show card B)

VI I U LI NI

ACADEMIC RESULTS
SOCIAL AND SPORTS FACILITIES
WIDE RANGE OF SUBJECTS
FRIENDLY ATMOSPHERE
DISCIPLINE
TIME TAKEN TO TRAVEL TO SCHOOL
EASE OF CONTACT BETWEEN YOURSELF AND
  TEACHERS
THE SCHOOLS REPUTATION
PARENTS VISITS AND OPEN EVENINGS

Q11   What would you regard as a good teacher?

Q12   Finally, could you please tell me the occupation of the
head of your household?

THANK YOU VERY MUCH FOR YOUR HELP.

Appendix D: Techniques for Measuring a School's Image

Familiarity – favourability analysis

This involves first establishing the extent of consumer awareness of the school's existence. Data is obtained by asking respondents to indicate the extent of their familiarity with a named school.

A possible format for recording respondent's reply is:

never heard of . . . . [ ]
heard of . . . . [ ]
know a little bit . . . . . . [ ]
know a fair amount . . . [ ]
know very well . . . . [ ]

Those respondents who *are aware* of the school are then invited to state the degree of their favourability towards it. A suggested format for noting reply is:

very unfavourable . . . . [ ]
somewhat unfavourable . . . [ ]
indifferent . . . . [ ]
somewhat favourable . . . . . [ ]
very favourable . . . . [ ]

This process is repeated for each school. The results are averaged and expressed in a two dimensional diagram where the schools are positioned in one of four categories according to how clients perceive them (figure D.1). Here, school A enjoys the strongest image, school B the weakest. Each requires different marketing strategies according to circumstances (figure D.2).

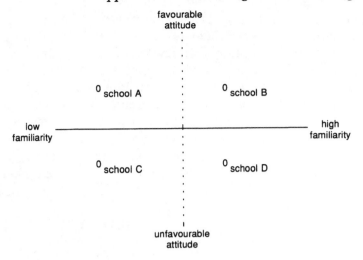

Figure D.1 Familiarity-favourability analysis
Source: Adapted from P. Kotler and Fox, *Strategic Marketing for Educational Institution*, Prentice Hall, Inc., Englewood Cliffs, New Jersey, 1985.

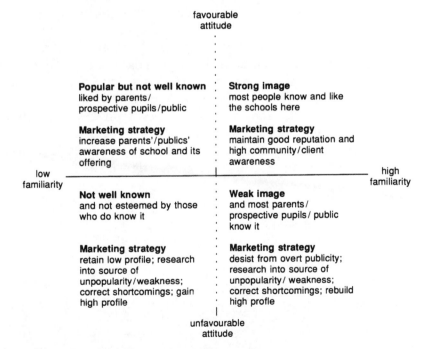

Figure D.2 Familiarity-favourability rating
Source: Adapted from Kotler and Fox, *Strategic Marketing for Educational Institutions*, 1985.

Respondents' familiarity – favourability with schools can be gauged more generally by asking them to identify as many institutions as possible, without prompting. And favourability towards each schools identified can be assessed by asking respondents to rank them, again unprompted, in order of preference. This approach benefits from spontaneity, but lacks a unit of measurement. Though useful, the results cannot be expressed in a two dimensional figure.

By undertaking familiarity – favourability analysis, a school can gain invaluable insight into the way consumers currently perceive it. But only two dimensions of image are revealed here. It is important also to flesh out or inject some content into consumers' perception of an institution.

Image profiling

The semantic differential will enable a school to create a descriptive image profile that facilitates comparison with competitors' features. These profiles reveal the basis by which clients choose one school in preference to rival institutions. This technique comprises two opposing adjectives which form a bipolar scale; for example 'academic'/'vocational', 'competitive'/'caring'. A list of relevant bipolar adjectives is compiled from market research data. Using a five point bipolar scale, respondents are asked to rate a specified school in terms of a number of listed adjectives. Averaging is used to convert responses to each adjectives to a single point on the scale (figure D.3). The process is repeated for each school and the results expressed on the same scale, thus facilitating comparison between the various institutions represented there (figure D.4).

To respondent

Please rate School A along the three attributes given below. Place an 'X' at the position on the scale that reflects your opinion.

Good reputation :_____:_____:__X__:_____:_____: poor reputation

Poor facilities   :_____:_____:_____:_____:__X__: good facilities

academic   :_____:__X__:_____:_____:_____: vocational

Figure D.3 Questionnaire extract: question using a group of three bipolar scales
Source: Kotler and Fox, *Strategic Marketing for Educational Institutions*, 1985.

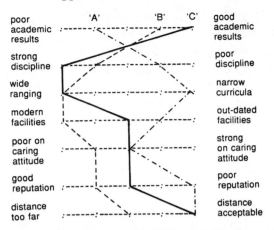

Figure D.4 Application of semantic differential scale to three competing schools in West Midlands
Source: Adapted from survey into marketing and schools, Birmingham Polytechnic Business School, 1988.

Another useful application of the semantic differential is in connection with position 'mapping'. Here, using the same principle as that for constructing a bipolar scale, respondents are asked to rank a number of specified, rival schools in terms of attributes they most closely associate with a good school. Responses are recorded on a five (or seven) point scale. A mean score is then computed and the results expressed on a continuum. The same procedure is employed to determine where respondents would position their ideal school, thus revealing the distance between it and other institutions covered in the survey (figure D.5). This process is repeated using another semantic differential. Here, respondents are asked to rate the same schools in terms of one other key attribute they associate with a good school, and to indicate an ideal position. Based on both sets of results, a two dimensional figure or positioning map, is attainable. Results for a recent market survey on behalf of a West Midlands school, illustrates the value of position mapping. The research found that parents judged academic results and disclines as the key factors when choosing schools (figure D.6). Three rival institutions are also indentified from the survey, including the map position of the ideal school. From the map, the institution which had commissioned the survey, school A, realized that its image is that of a more academically successful school than rival D, comparable to C in this respect, but inferior to D. But A's reputation for discipline is unrivalled except by B. Clearly, A's most serious threat is B whose image in more favourable on both counts and whose position is closest to the ideal. A number of possible marketing strategies to help A improve its public image are evident: undertake market research to determine why B is perceived so much better in terms of the two criteria, take stock of current PR activities and improve, check and correct behaviour of pupils, and so on.

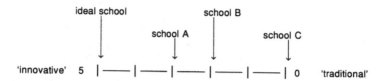

Figure D.5 Positions plotted on a continuum

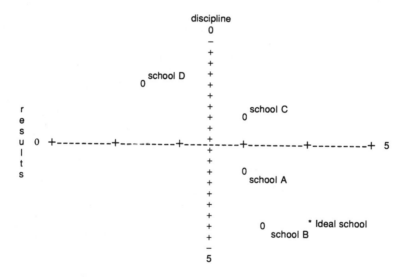

Figure D.6 Recent survey into schools in West Midlands: parent's perceptions expressed via position map
Source: School survey, Birmingham Polytechnic Business School, 1988.

This activity might be repeated periodically to ascertain how much closer a school is perceived to be by one or more market segments to their ideal institution; the SPSSx statistical package is available to assist with this analysis. Depending on outcome, the school's marketing strategy may need adjusting in order to reposition it *vis-à-vis* competitors and the best.

The semantic differential, then, is a useful tool in added content to the familiarity – favourability image scale. While this approach does have its limitations (it is not, for example, recommended for overall attitude measurement), it is appropriate for image-descriptive purposes. Indeed, this method has the advantage of general validity, simplicity, versatility, speed, and produces results that are comparable to those of more complex scaling methods.

Appendix E: Marketing Education Services Overseas

Introduction

Northfield Mount Hermon School in Massachusetts, USA, has developed since its inception over 100 years ago, strong links with overseas education markets. Indeed, today, over 30 per cent of its 1,000 boarders are international students or offspring of Americans living abroad. In sizeable numbers, Northfield Mount Hermon recruits young people from Belgium, West Germany, Hong Kong, United Arab Emirates, Venezuela and 60 other overseas countries. And many other schools serve similar markets. By what method(s) might a boarding school or sixth form or further education college market their products overseas? This chapter offers some useful hints, supported by a case study (based on recent experience of a British college which undertook overseas marketing).

Formulating Strategies for Overseas Marketing

Commonality of marketing principles

In formulating strategies for overseas marketing, account must be taken of the planning process described earlier in the book (see chapter 3). Indeed, many key activities associated with planning for a domestic market are relevant to overseas marketing: undertaking market research to identify overseas opportunities, setting goals and objectives against which marketing activities can be appraised, formulating marketing strategies (via the marketing mix), creating appropriate and responsive internal communication and carefully planning and managing the marketing processes. The principles on which these activities are based apply to domestic and overseas marketing alike.

Peculiarities of overseas marketing

Notwithstanding, some aspects of domestic marketing may be inappropriate for the overseas situation. Marketing mix strategies, for example, may need modifying for each overseas market. Moreover, owing to differences in culture and language, key marketing activities such as research and corporate and product advertising are more complex and difficult to undertake in overseas countries than in the domestic market.

Researching overseas markets

In order to make a correct assessment of marketing opportunities in an overseas country and the accessibility of the market there, and decide an appropriate marketing mix strategy, thorough research must be undertaken. As for domestic marketing, desk and field research are appropriate here (see chapter 5).

Desk research will help elicit relevant information on those overseas countries of interest to a school/college. While there are many such sources, some of the more obvious ones are the British Council, the Market Research Society in the UK, Export Market Information Centre at Warwick University, UK, Department of Trade and Industry Export Market Information Centre in London, and so on. The Market Research Society's publication *Country Notes* provides demographic data, research procedures and sources of information, and media influences in countries such as China, Hong Kong, Indonesia, Japan, Malaysia, Nepal, Singapore, Thailand, and so on.[1] Moreover, the Market Research Society, in conjunction with Industrial Marketing Research Association, publishes a free introductory guide for schools who wish to carry out their own initial exploratory research. This guide identifies relevant information and indicates where to find it.[2] Other key sources include the UN Demographic Yearbook which is available from large reference libraries, World Advertising Expenditure which identifies media influences overseas and is obtainable from the UK Advertising Association[3]. Desk research enables a school to learn much about the country from where they intend recruiting often without incurring any cost.

Field research is also important here. Interviews with British Council officials and representatives, specially convened field trips to feeder schools in overseas countries, discussion with visitors to education exhibitions overseas, are some suitable means of gathering primary data. To facilitate field research, a school or college can apply for an Export Market Research Grant from the Association of British Chamber of Commerce; grants were formerly administered by the Department of Trade and Industry. The grant of half of the overseas travel costs enables a school or college to send one representative overseas to conduct a market research survey, though overt promotion of a school is not permitted. Two projects are allowed in each calendar year. Many of the market research techniques and approaches which are described and analyzed in chapter 5, are highly pertinent to collecting secondary and primary sources of data.

Planning and organizing exploratory visits to potential overseas markets

Speculative visits and Britain's Department of Trade and Industry funded visits need to be carefully planned. Itineraries need to be prepared well in advance and contacts obtained prior to the visit. A detailed report needs to be kept of the visit and this may require the college representative to write up copious notes after each day spent overseas. Information needs to be sifted and often acted upon during the visit. The college representative needs to be of sufficient seniority to be able to make decisions and negotiate fees and commissions on the spot, if necessary.

Marketing mix strategies

As argued earlier in the book (see chapter 3), the implementation of marketing strategy is undertaken via the marketing mix. Here, the various elements of the marketing mix, i.e. product, price, place and promotion, must be prioritized to suit the market conditions in which a school operates. An appropriate mix of product, price, place and promotion must be adopted for each country from which the school/college wishes to recruit.

Each element of the marketing mix comprises a number of specific activities. Figure E. 1 identifies a number of activities especially relevant to overseas marketing.

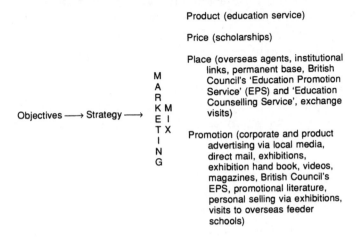

Product (education service)

Price (scholarships)

Place (overseas agents, institutional links, permanent base, British Council's 'Education Promotion Service' (EPS) and 'Education Counselling Service', exchange visits)

Objectives ⟶ Strategy ⟶ MARKETING MIX

Promotion (corporate and product advertising via local media, direct mail, exhibitions, exhibition hand book, videos, magazines, British Council's EPS, promotional literature, personal selling via exhibitions, visits to overseas feeder schools)

Figure E.1 Marketing mix for overseas markets

Most of these activities are presented and critically discussed earlier in the book. Some which are especially relevant to overseas marketing are described below. The success of an overseas marketing mix strategy is dependent on the assimulation of the various mix elements into the overseas culture – it cannot be simply bolted on to a school's domestic mix strategy – and the mutual support and underpinning which each element gives the other.

Corporate/Product Advertising and Distribution Overseas

The growing emphasis on corporate publicity and corporate advertising in education marketing generally, is reflected in the weight of material expounded in chapters 9 and 10. And this priority applies also to overseas marketing where media advertising, direct mail, magazine advertising and exhibitions form the main vehicles for targeting messages on relevant audiences. All four activities are described below, in the context of the overseas market. Detailed considerations are omitted here since earlier chapters deal with these aspects of the material.

Local advertising media

Much of the earlier discussion on the use of media for the purpose of corporate publicity, corporate advertising and product advertising are relevant hear. But a number of important considerations peculiar to overseas marketing need emphasizing or reiterating.

First, a college's/school's overseas corporate advertising must be reinforced by promotion activities such as exhibitions or visits, i.e. personal selling. As a general rule, as argued earlier in the book (see chapter 10), the effectiveness of corporate advertising derives from the mutual support and underpinning it receives from other elements in the communication mix.

Second, guidance concerning issues relating to language, suitability or cultural acceptance of advertising in a specified overseas country, choice of media outlet for advertising and the identity of an agent to place the advertisment, must be sought. The British Council may be able to help in these matters.

In this context, UK magazines or 'glossies' with distribution outlets overseas may be worth considering as vehicles for advertising education services. Magazines sometimes permit editorials alongside advertisements and are especially useful for reaching fragmented markets such as those in the Middle East.

Direct mail

This is another appropriate promotion activity for overseas marketing. It is worth noting that to maximize the benefit of direct mail in overseas marketing, it is often helpful to establish a PO Box in the country concerned. This will promote a more convenience method for consumer replies and facilitate an easier collection of responses.

Posters

These are also useful for advertising education services overseas. Strategically placed to reach the target audience, posters can be highly effective means of advertising. They are also comparatively inexpensive *vis-à-vis* many other forms of advertising and can be displayed over a long period of time. But the use of large poster displays demands thorough understanding of the country's culture, language and its institutions. Moreover, the danger of overkill is ever present.

Exhibition handbooks

Handbooks which accompany overseas exhibitions are effective vehicles for advertising education products. The British Council recently organized an exhibition for further and higher education in Hong Kong, which took place in November 1989. In order to promote the event, the British Council produced and widely distributed an exhibition handbook. Those UK education institutions intending to participate in the exhibition were offered advertising space in the publication – a key opportunity to reach target audiences. The cost for placing a full, one-page advertisment in the Hong Kong handbook was about £400.

Exhibitions

Participating in exhibitions requires many hours of preparation and considerable investment in terms of human and physical resources since staff will be required to travel abroad.

While schools/colleges must undertake much of the initial planning and resource investment themselves, exhibition organizers do contribute here: they usually provide booth space at the exhibition, where the school/college will display its materials and from which it can publicize its products, they often provide a travel and accommodation packages, and as a rule provide briefings about the exhibition, both in the UK and overseas, in the run-up period.

If a school/college is to maximize its investment in an exhibition, a number of key rules need to be observed:

- every aspect of the exhibition must be scrupulously planned well in advance of the exhibition date, and certainly prior to staff travelling overseas
- all staff manning the school's/college's exhibition stand must be well briefed

- all literature/brochures to be distributed at the exhibition stand must take account of the language and culture of the host country (simply using materials designed for the domestic market may be inappropriate)
- it is helpful to have staff member at school/college as point-of-contact should overseas team need urgent assistance or information
- testimonials written by alumni from the country where the exhibition is being held, and written in the country's language, can be distributed to visitors to the exhibition stand – (this type of activity has proved an especially effective means of corporate and product advertising in Japan)
- on completion of the exhibition, an evaluation of its effectiveness and contribution to the realization of the school's/college's objectives must be undertaken

Overseas agents

An alternative for colleges marketing overseas is to appoint an agent or representative in the overseas country. Some UK colleges have adopted this approach, particularly where the British Council's Education Promotion Service does not have a significant presence. Appointing an agent requires considerable consideration and care. The British Council generally does not approve of colleges appointing agents, but if they are consulted during the selection process, they can provide some useful pointers. In some countries agents charge a fee to the college on each student enrolled, in other words, the student pays the fee to the agent. In others the agent makes his income either from providing travel services to the student or from selling publications on studying abroad. An alternative is to appoint a representative overseas, possibly a retired headteacher, to act on behalf of the college. In some countries agents have a poor reputation with parents, particularly resulting from the action of some Australian agents.

Education Promotion and Education Counselling Services

In 1988, the British Council launched the Education Promotion Service (EPS) to coordinate overseas marketing of further education. Within a short period, the EPS had established representation in two key markets for further education: Hong Kong and Malaysia. Today, the EPS has extended its activities to many more countries of interest to schools and colleges involved in overseas marketing, and further expansion is envisaged. The Education Counselling Service (ECS) undertakes a similar role for higher education.

To obtain any real benefit from joining the EPS, a college needs to participate annually in one or more of the exhibitions either organized or supported by the British Council and be marketing full-time courses. Courses such as A levels, Access courses and BTEC Diplomas can be promoted very successfully through EPS.

Institutional links

Another useful mechanism for marketing overseas is the development of one-to-one institutional links with an educational institution in the country where they seek to recruit. This might involve students taking the first year of a two-year course in their home country, where staff from a UK school or college undertake some teaching, and completing the final year of the course in the UK institution. This reduces the tuition fees to students from overseas, many of whom need scholarships to study overseas, and helps staff develop necessary expertise in overseas marketing. This linking technique is particularly popular in Malaysia and Brunei.

Permanent base

This helps promote the distribution of education services to overseas markets. It also assists schools to become more easily assimilated into the culture of a foreign country, thus enhancing the effectiveness of its advertising there. It can, however, make considerable demands on a school's resources.

Videos and promotional literature

During visits and missions to overseas countries, videos, prospectuses and promotional literature can be shown/distributed to prospects with great effect. Such materials are also invaluable at exhibitions and visits to overseas feeder schools.

Case study Filton College Bristol: A Strategy for Marketing Overseas[4]

Filton College in Bristol, UK, was open in 1960 and 30 years later is catering for approximately 1,500 full-time and 2,500 part-time students. Courses are offered in four departments: arts, business studies and management, mathematics, science and technology and social studies.

Filton College has always enrolled a significant number of overseas students. The British Council contracted with the college to provide full-time engineering courses for students from the Oman and elsewhere in the Middle East, during the latter part of the 1970s. This work supplemented the European students who came to the College for full-time and part-time one-year English as a Foreign Language courses. Overseas recruitment onto vocational courses had always been far more sporadic, with only single figure enrolments on full-time business studies and A level GCE courses.

The spur to begin marketing overseas came from a decline in the work for the British Council's Omani students. The Oman had, by the mid-1980s, built its own technical training establishment and was no longer sending groups of students overseas to study. In addition, staff at Filton became aware of the more aggressive marketing being undertaken by both state and independent colleges of further education. Following discussions among a number of interested staff, a paper was presented to the Principal outlining a rudimentary marketing strategy for recruiting overseas students. This involved re-naming the existing EFL Centre, the Overseas Students Centre, which would then become the focus of all the college's overseas work. This resulted in the centre also becoming the focus of all overseas students interviewing and admissions. The Centre became the information point for any college department which needed advice on overseas student affairs.

Education Promotion Service

At about the same time, Filton College took a policy decision to join EPS for an initial period of three years, after which it was agreed a thorough review of this investment would take place. The annual subscription of £5,000–£7,500 for the first year – was paid, which resulted in Filton becoming a full member and not part of any wider consortium of colleges, a mechanism which has recently become popular. An immediate but unexpected benefit for the college was that Filton was featured in a British Council Video entitled *Studying in the UK*. Not only was Filton College mentioned by name, but the college obtained, at no charge, the raw video-tape shot by the makers of the Council's video. This was later used as the basis for the college's own overseas marketing video, a production lasting 12 minutes and used at exhibitions and in British Council offices overseas.

Exhibitions

Filton's first exhibition was in Kuala Lumpur. To prepare staff for the proposed visit and generate interest in it, a small working group was convened for the purpose. The group's membership was comprised of three senior staff, assisted where necessary by the college's Marketing Coordinator and technical experts, such as graphic designers and printers.

The working group held briefings for the whole college staff about the proposed visit and its objectives. As a result a number of staff began to express an interest in overseas work, perhaps because of the chance to travel overseas, but more often because of a genuine interest in such a development. The overseas marketing group finally requested that the Principal choose who would travel overseas to represent the college, after taking representations from the group. A consideration for the group was that an overseas visit places a great test upon the two college representatives – Filton had already agreed that a minimum of two representatives would travel to each exhibition. They needed to be able to work together successfully both personally and professionally. If one member took ill during a visit, the other one would have to minister to them, requiring considerable interpersonal skills. In addition the rigours of travelling overseas required that college representatives have considerable reserves of stamina and energy.

The most crucial first step for the college was producing a Gantt Chart of the tasks to be undertaken and the deadlines by which they had to be completed, in preparation for the visit. As the date of the exhibition approached the planning of deadlines became more critical. The greater the number of tasks that could be completed in the early stages, the easier the final preparations.

At Filton the first problem was to obtain the funds necessary to facilitate the appearance at the exhibition. The college was fortunate in having a commitment from its Principal of up to £7,500, but with the strict proviso that it kept copious details of all of its expenditure. Apart from the cost of air travel and accommodation, the two biggest items of expenditure were a portable display stand, which could be taken as carry-on baggage on the plane and a publicity pack, designed specifically for the overseas market. The display stand, which eventually cost in excess of £2,500, proved most successful. The college's photography section took a range of shots of activities in the college and these were incorporated by the stand's manufacturers into the final version. Early on the college adopted a logo specifically for the overseas market – namely Concorde – and this proved to be a wise choice. The display stand featured a large photograph of Concorde landing at Filton – the college is next door to Rolls Royce and British Aerospace – and this was most arresting as visitors to the exhibition walked past Filton's stand.

The publicity material consisted of single sheets describing each course the college was promoting overseas, presented in an attractive high quality folder. This meant that only a dozen or so courses were described in detail. One of the overseas team acted as editor and worked through the literature prior to typesetting to ensure that the language was readily understandable by potential students from overseas. The college has since abandoned the single sheet literature in favour of a book containing the same information. The problems of collating the sheets and handling them on what was sometimes a very busy stand proved difficult. Filton also purchased plastic display stands for leaflets to use as point-of-sale material. These were damaged en route to Kuala Lumpur and now all of the college's publicity material and items to be sent abroad are packed in tea chests, not cardboard boxes, and sent by air and sea freight. The advantage of air freight is that despatch dates are later than those for sea freight, giving longer preparation time.

The college's representatives were provided with a range of other materials. The college produced 5,000 single sheet leaflets which could be given to visitors passing the college's stand – the high quality publicity packs (of which 2,500 were sent to Kuala Lumpur) were reserved for only the most interested visitors – plus smaller numbers of home publicity material. The college also obtained letters of greeting to the people of Kuala Lumpur from the mayors of the County of Avon, City of Bristol and District of Northavon. These were displayed in the booth alongside the college's display stand and proved very useful assets. The college's photographic section produced a range of photographs mounted on polystyrene boards, including shots of the types of accommodation overseas students use during their stay at Filton and shots of Bristol and the college. A video of the college is a useful tool and, using British Council footage, plus tape shot by college audio-visual staff, was incorporated into a video, with commentary.

This video has now been copied into overseas tape formats and copies deposited with educational agents and careers teachers overseas. The college plans to produce more comprehensive information packs for careers teachers overseas and for educational agents. Both of these groups may be vital in obtaining overseas students for a college or school.

Perhaps the most crucial part of the pre-exhibition preparation was the briefing of those staff manning the stand. Everyone in a college knows what their own department has to offer, but they do not necessarily know what course offerings other departments have.

These briefings took up to three full days, but proved invaluable. Departments within the college were able to provide our representatives with a wide range of supporting information and details on former overseas students who had succeeded at the college.

This information is vital, particularly in the Japanese market, where recommendation of a college or course by an existing Japanese student is of considerable value. Many colleges now take testimonials written in the native language with them overseas. In future the college plans to use a portable computer to take abroad details of past students and details of all the courses the college offers, both at home and overseas. Filton also plans to use the portable computer to log enquiries, as these may run into many hundreds during the course of a four-day exhibition. Some colleges have actively developed overseas alumni associators, and students from these associations help represent the college on the stand during the exhibition. The college is currently considering forming such an alumni. The local office of the English Tourist Board provided us with posters and brochures about Bristol. This helped the college to promote Bristol, using the non-educational benefits of the city. The culture and history of the UK is still a strong selling point overseas.

Filton College also decided to have a member of staff back at the college available at short notice to deal with any problems that occurred for the team overseas, such as sickness, loss of currency, etc. Initially staff from the college did not have a corporate American Express account and found this presented significant problems. As a result, each member of college staff travelling overseas has a college credit card, currently American Express, soon to be changed to Visa for greater acceptabilty. The college has had to produce detailed expenditure guidelines and procedures and have them agreed by both college senior management and the representatives of the local education authority. It has proved a wise investment of time.

Post-exhibition action

The overseas marketing group agreed from the outset that once an exhibition was over it was necessary to produce a detailed report, really to act as an action plan for future exhibitions. After the college's first exhibition in Kuala Lumpur it found it had made no fatal errors in preparation, but some fine tuning of specific items was necessary, such as publicity material and the packaging and shipping of items for the exhibition. Also all enquiries needed to be followed up, preferably with a personalized letter to the potential student. Action needed to be taken on any enquiries for courses which were offered in other colleges. Good relations can be built up between seemingly competing organizations this way.

Agents

Another element in Filton's overseas marketing strategy was the use of agents, particularly in those countries where the British Council's Education Promotion Service does not have a significant presence.

Filton's future overseas marketing strategy

The college's future marketing activities will involve undertaking a number of initiatives. The first involves market research. In this connection, Filton has recently obtained an Export Market Research Grant which has so far facilitated two overseas trips with a third planned for the near future. And a second initiative involves establishing formal links with overseas colleges, possibly in Malaysia where such activities bring considerable mutual benefits to participants.

Key points

1 While many aspects of overseas marketing are similar to those found in domestic marketing, there are important differences. For example:

- marketing mix strategies need to be modified for each overseas market;
- full account must be taken of cultural and language differences in under taking, among other things, corporate and product advertising.

2 Desk and field research are important to schools in their search for overseas marketing opportunities.
3 Speculative overseas visits must be carefully planned well in advance.
4 In implementing a marketing mix strategy, a number of promotion and distribution activities are especially relevant for overseas:

- advertising in local media
- using direct mail
- advertising via poster
- advertising in exhibition handbook
- participating in exhibitions
- using the British Council's Education Promotion and Counselling Services
- establishing institutional links with overseas schools
- setting up a permanent overseas base
- using videos and promotional literature

Notes

1 *Country Notes*, The Market Research Society, London, UK.

2 'International Desk Research: An Introductory Guide' (leaflet), The Market Research Society and Industrial Marketing Research Association, undated.

3 Available from The Advertising Association, Abford House, 15 Wilton Street, London, SW1V 1NJ.

4 This case study was written by John Parnham.

Index